Beautiful Feathers

A Bird Coloring Book for Adults

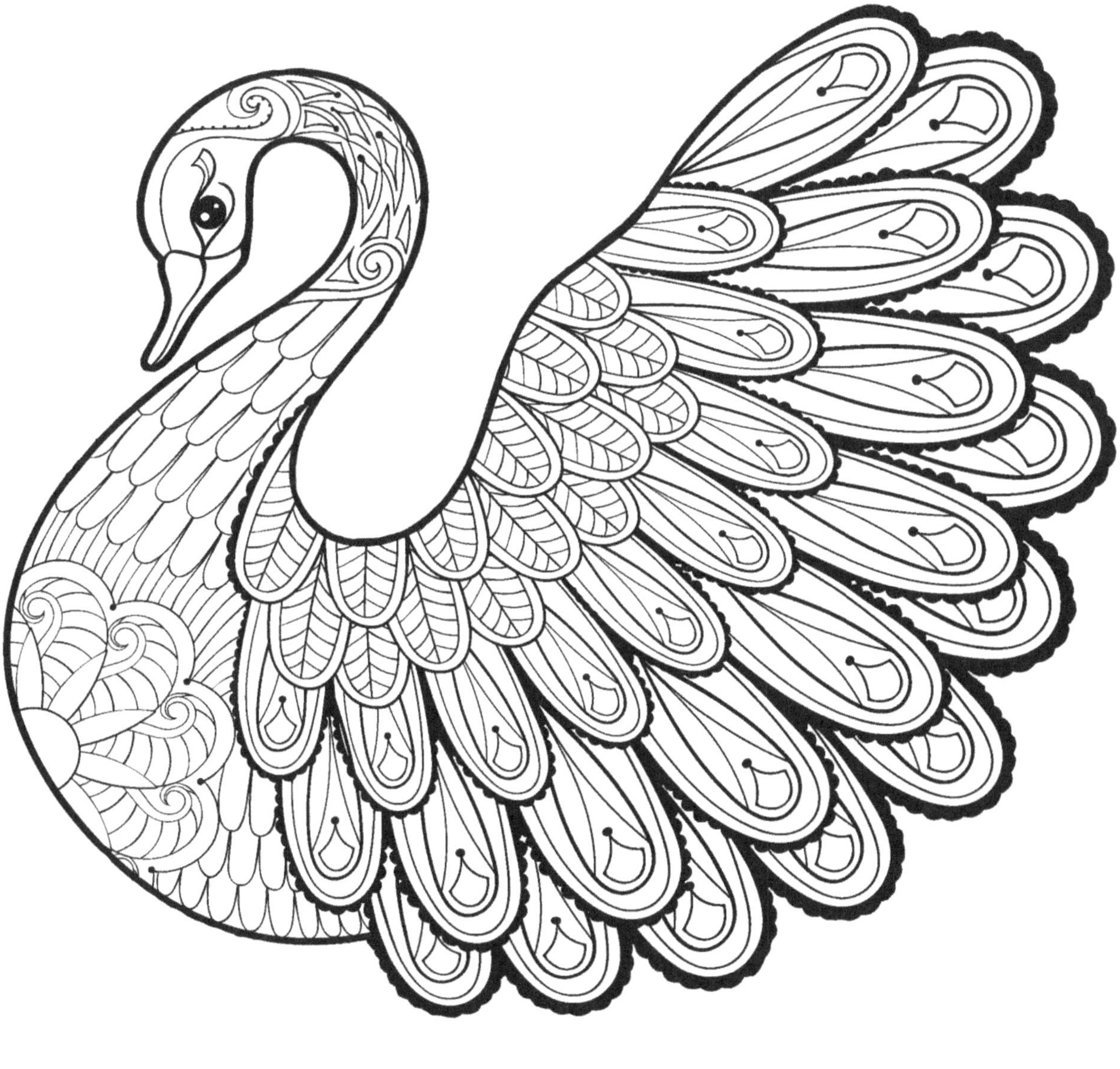

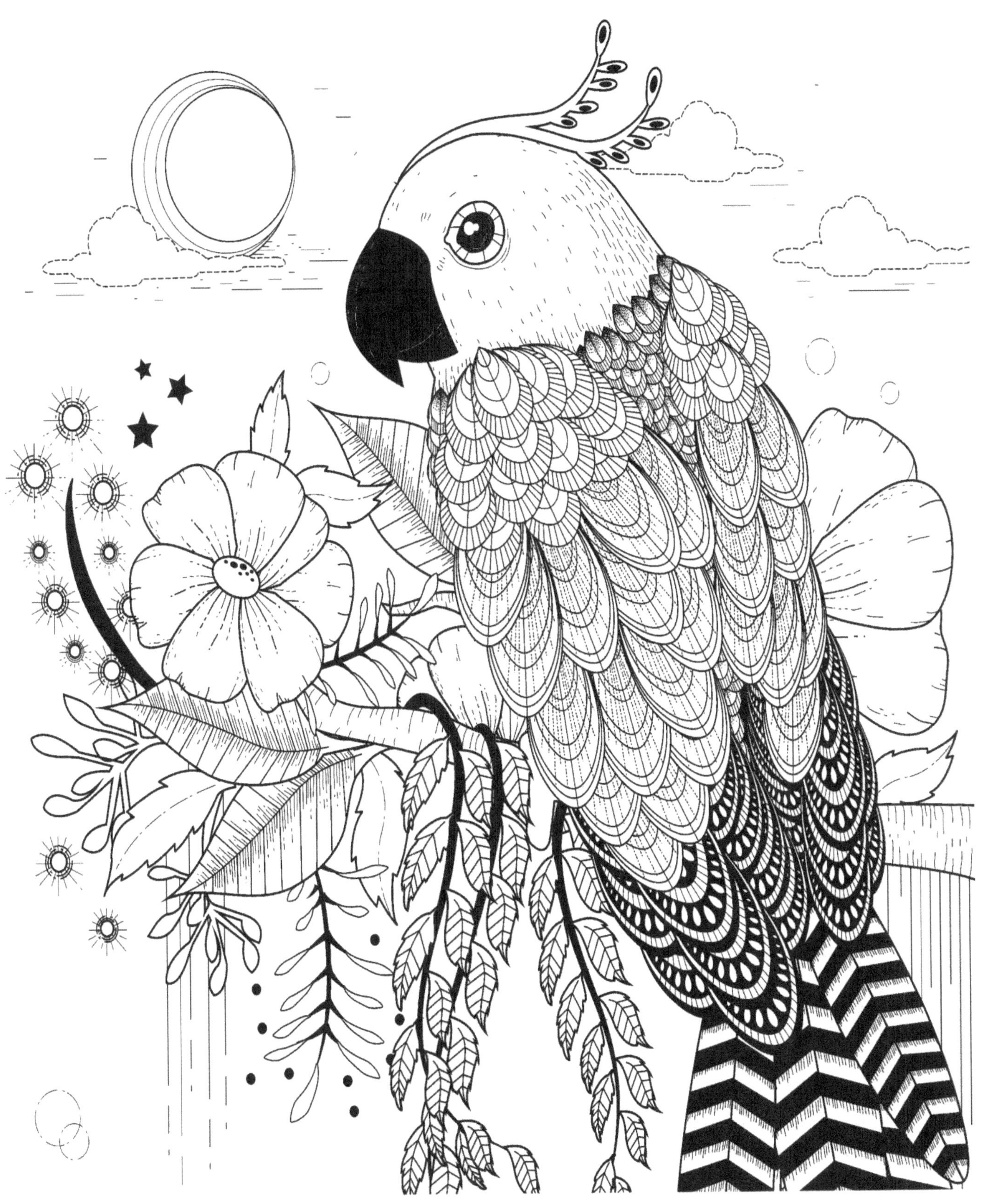

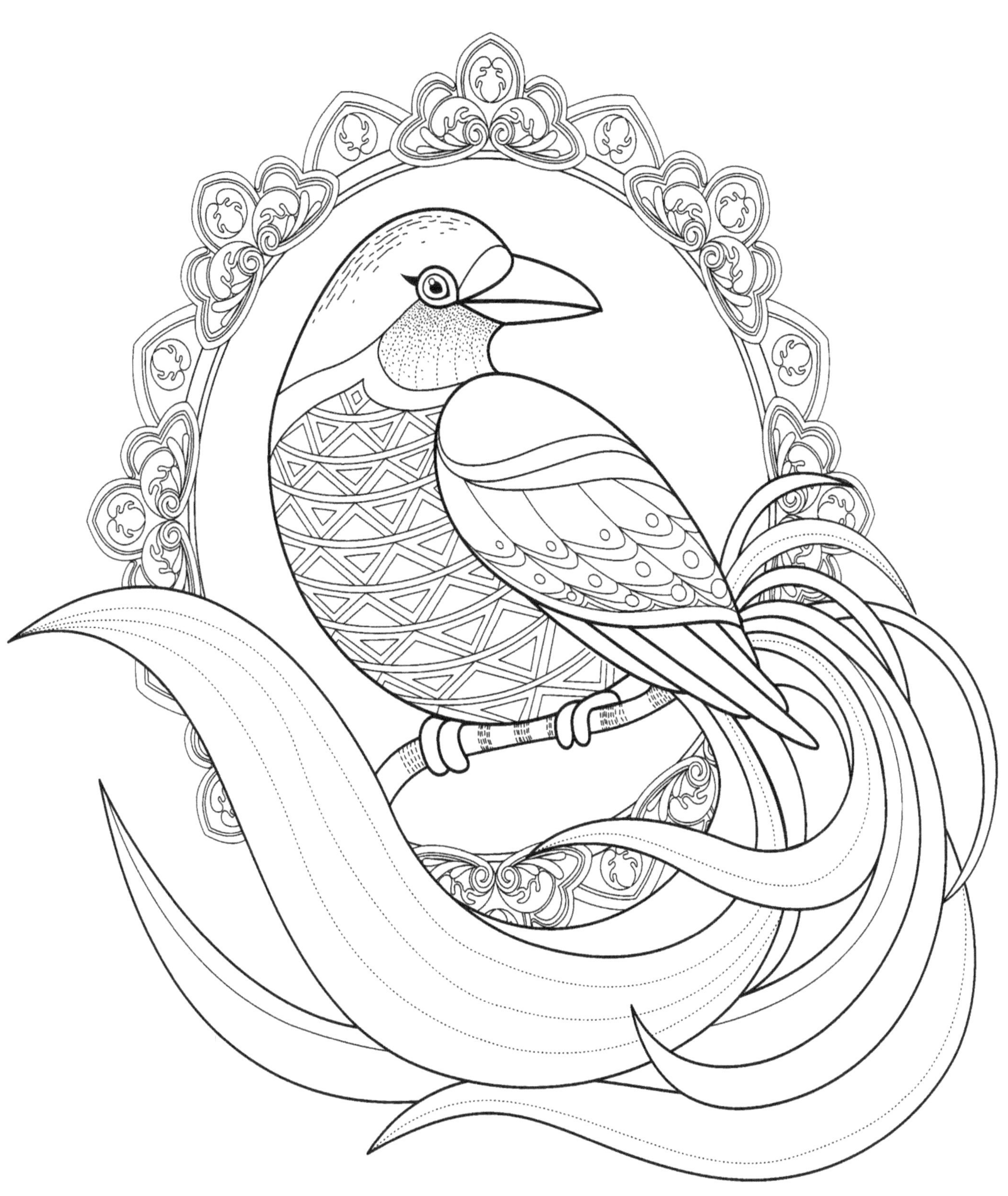

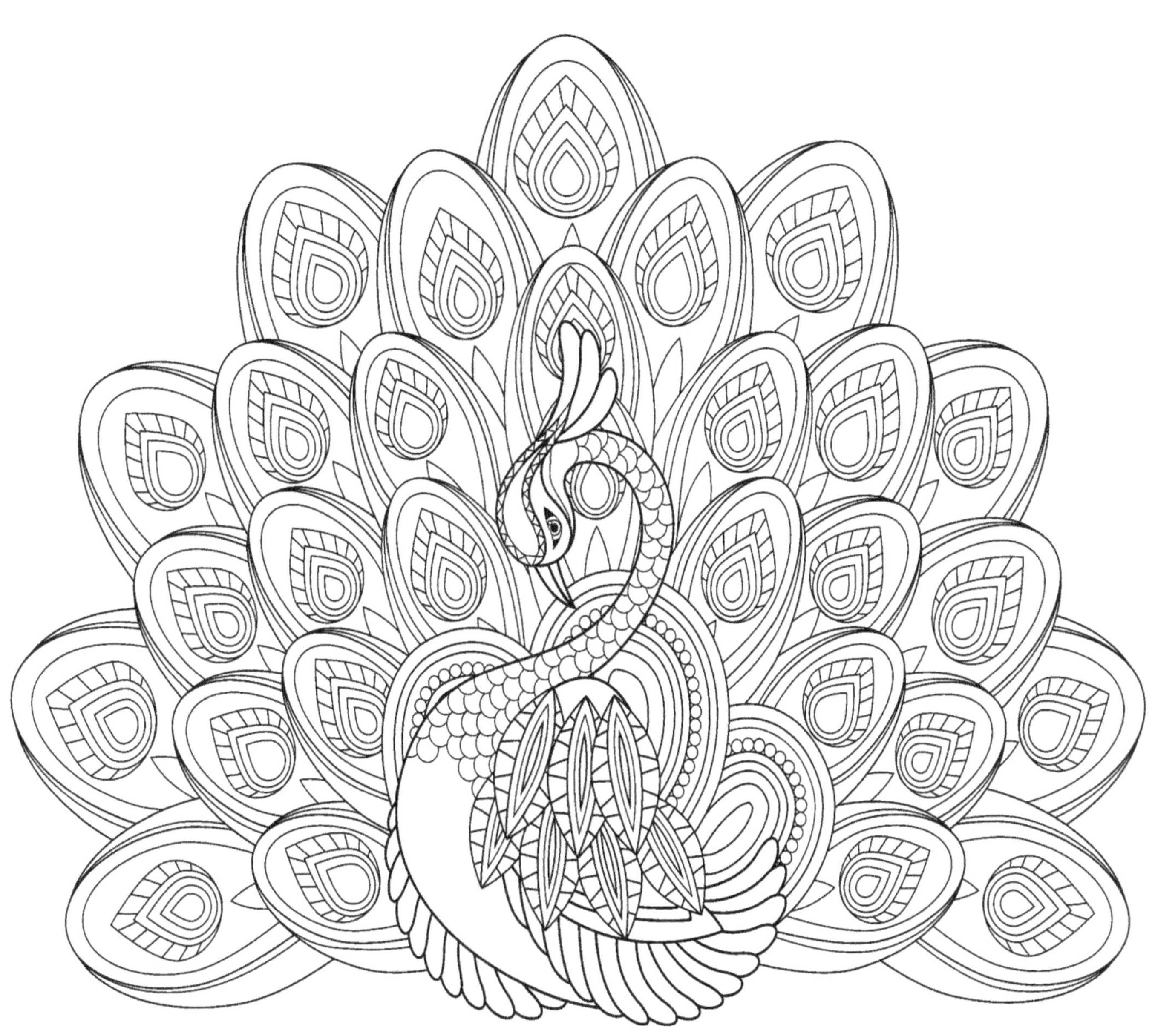

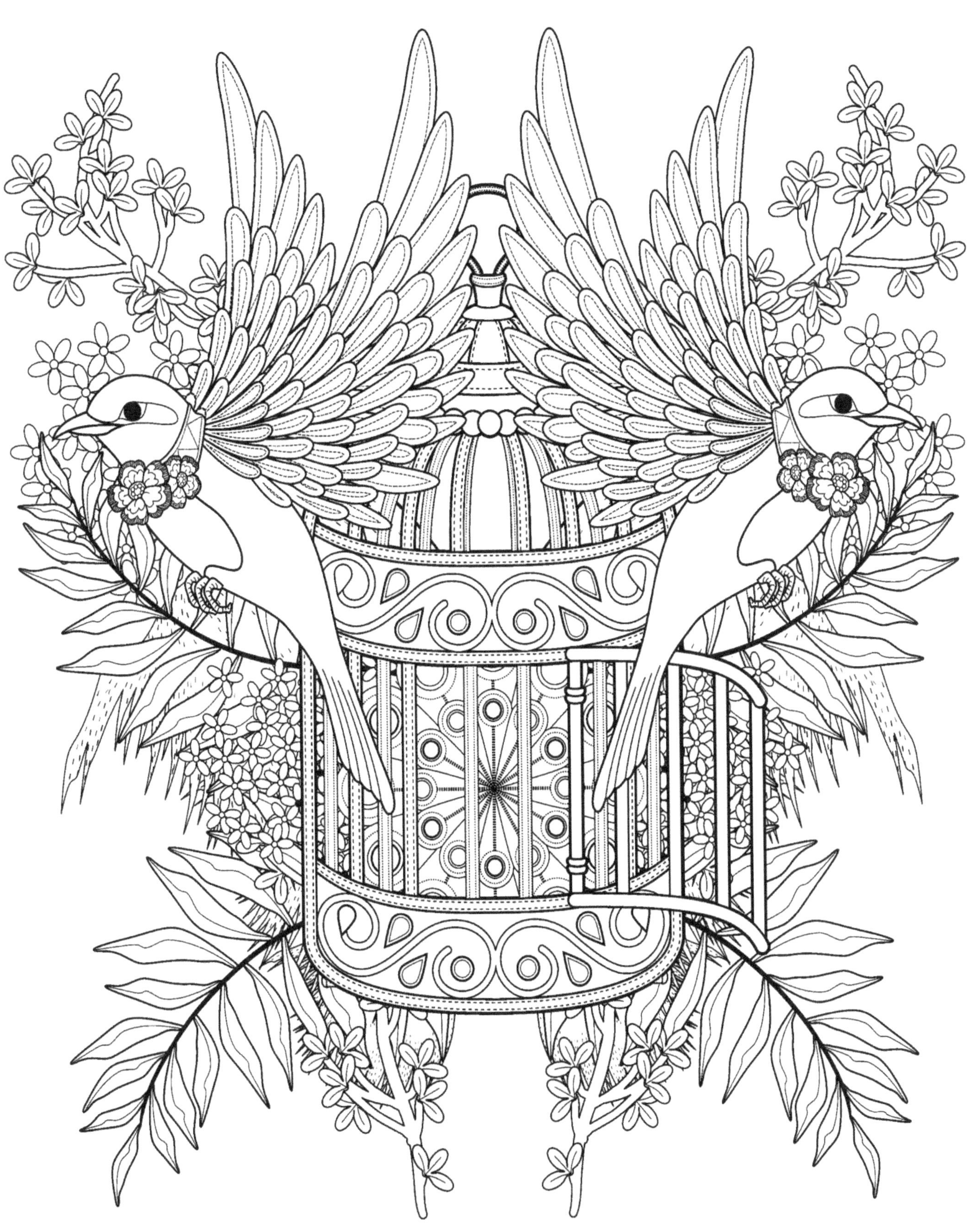

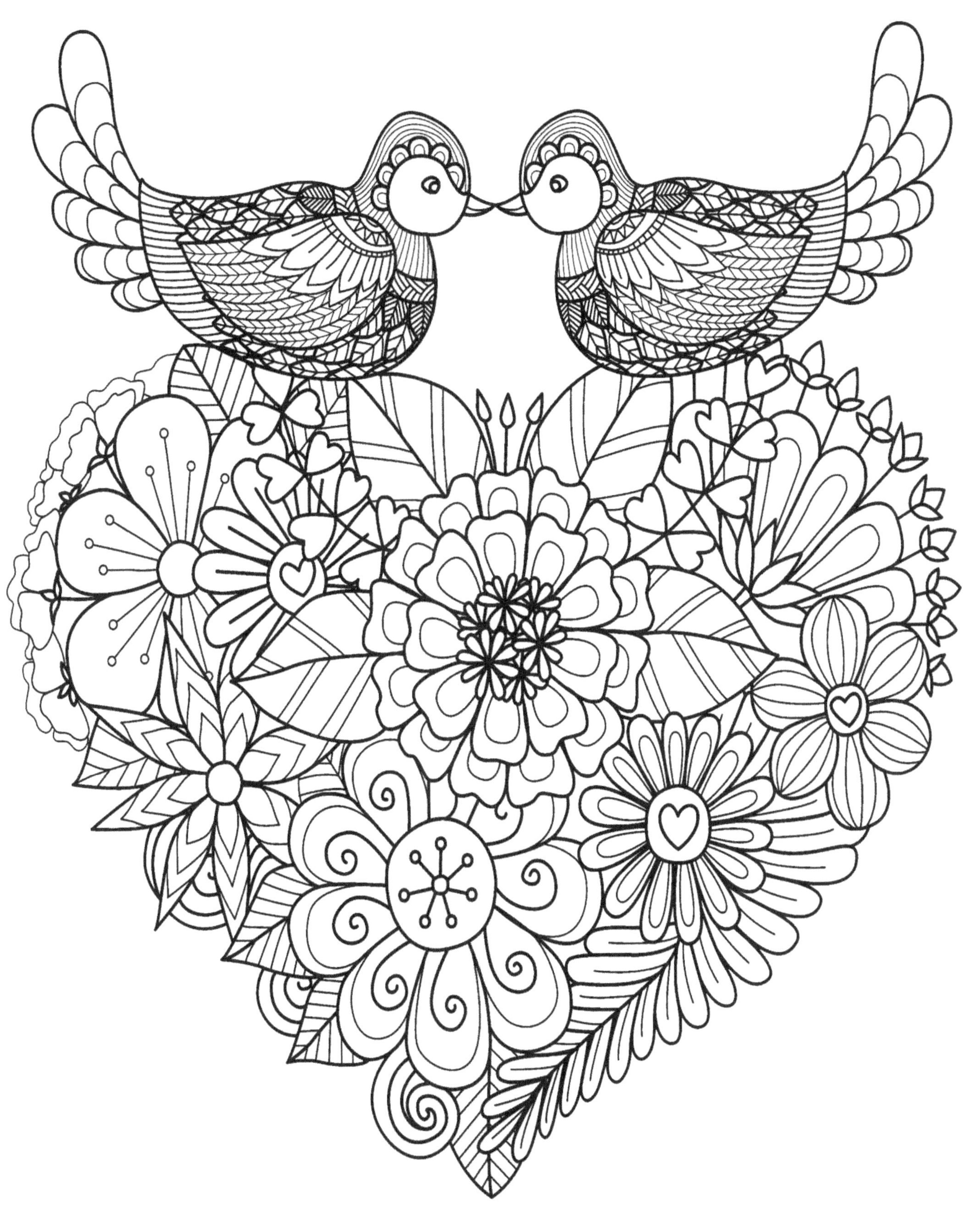

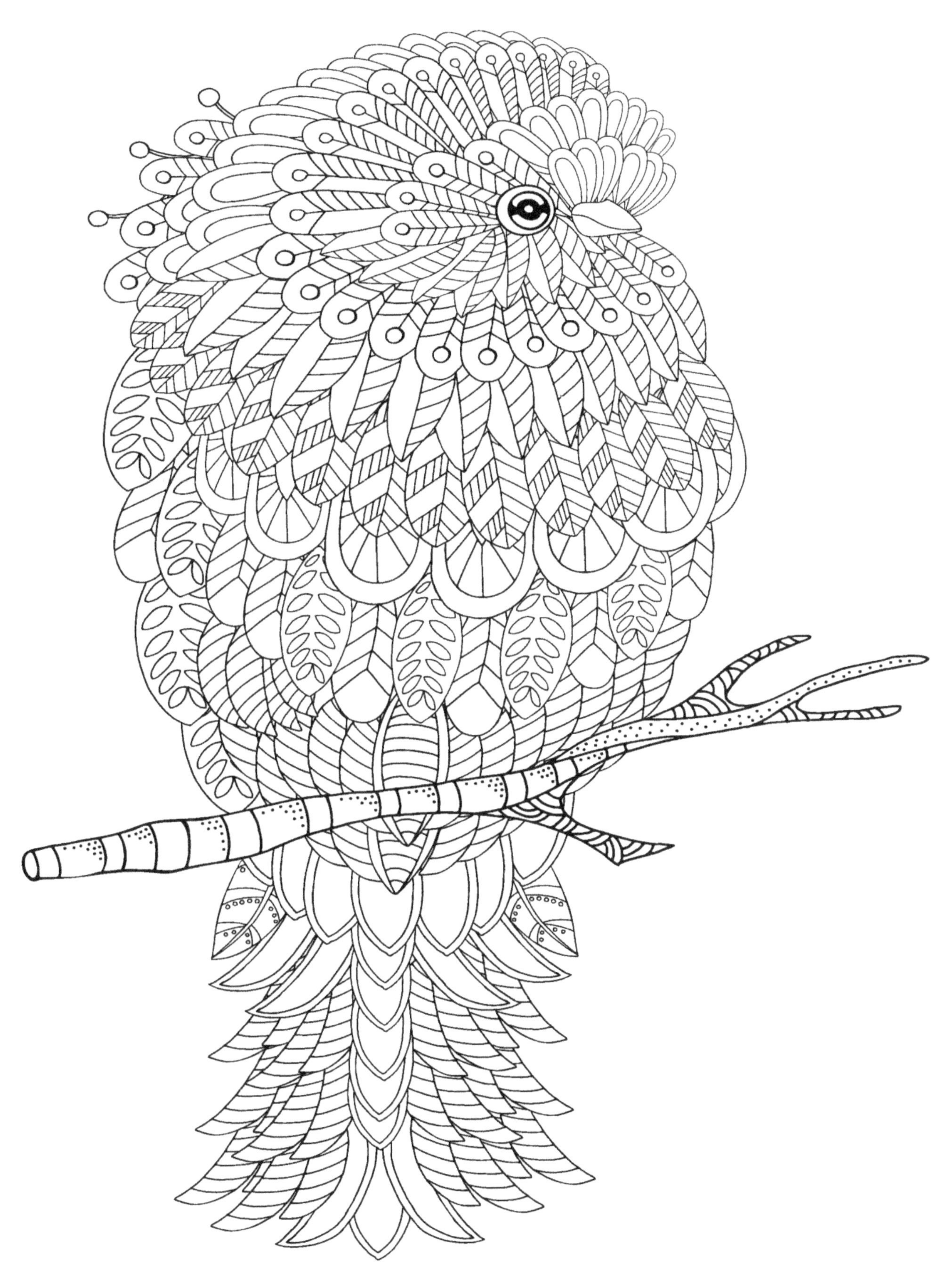

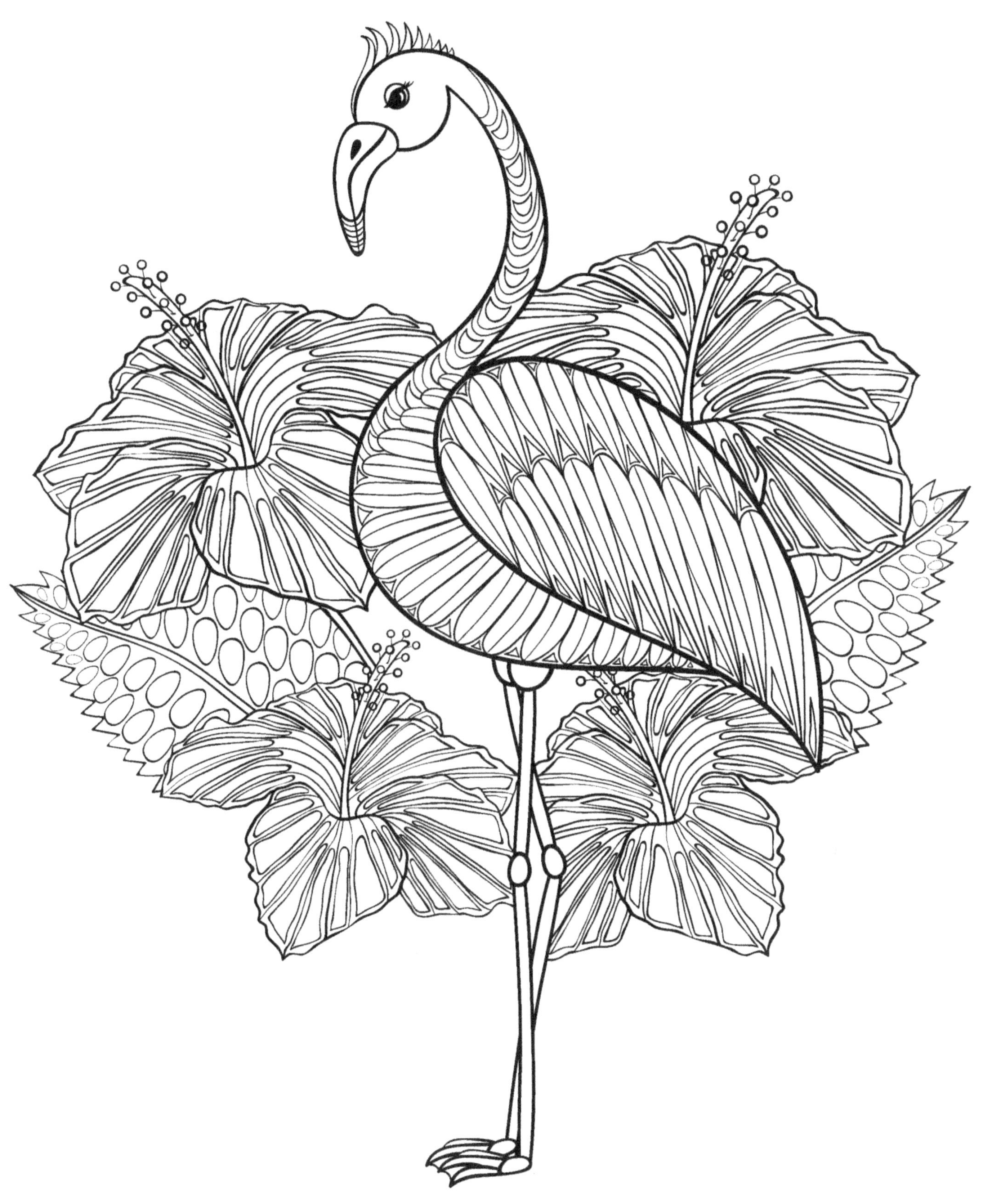

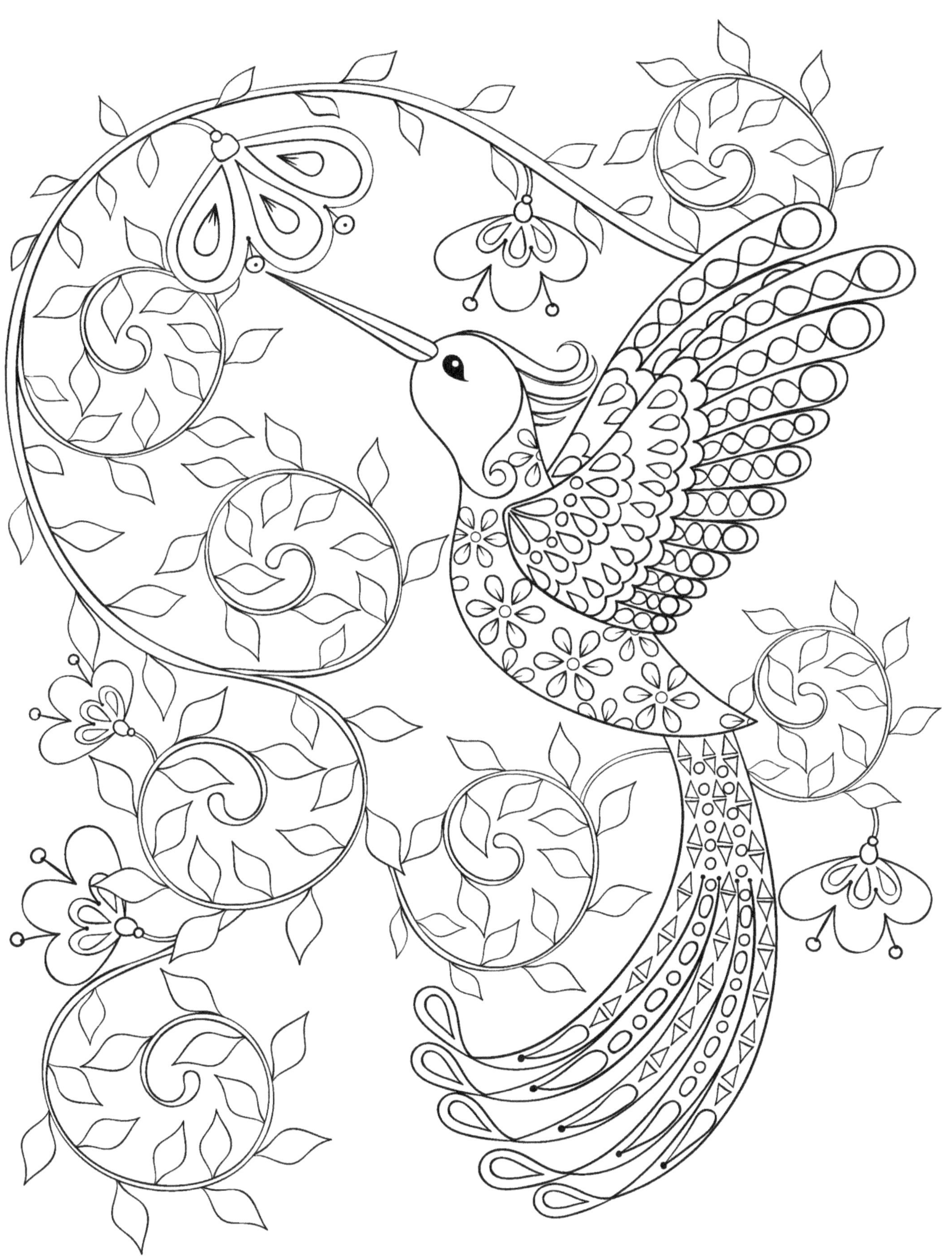

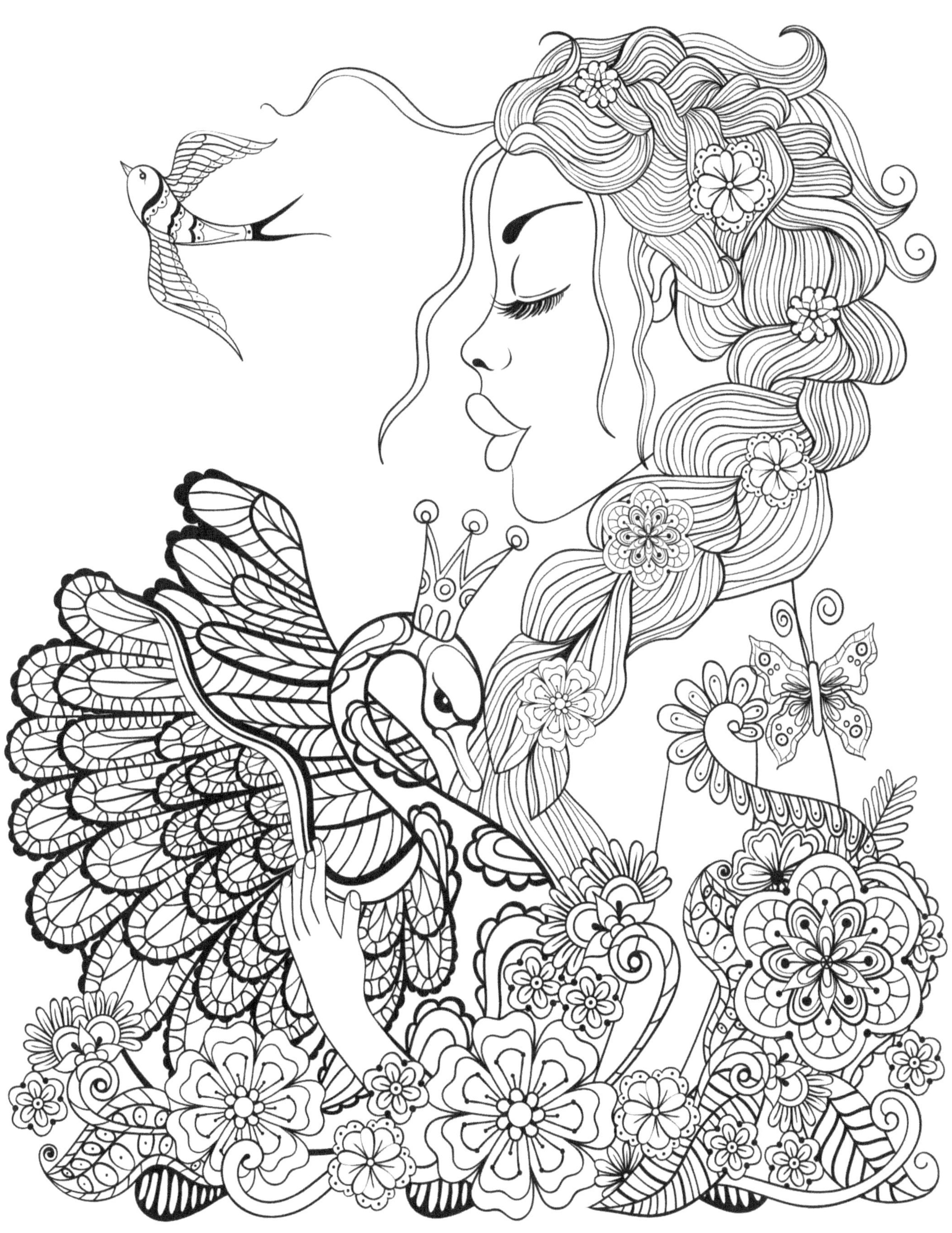

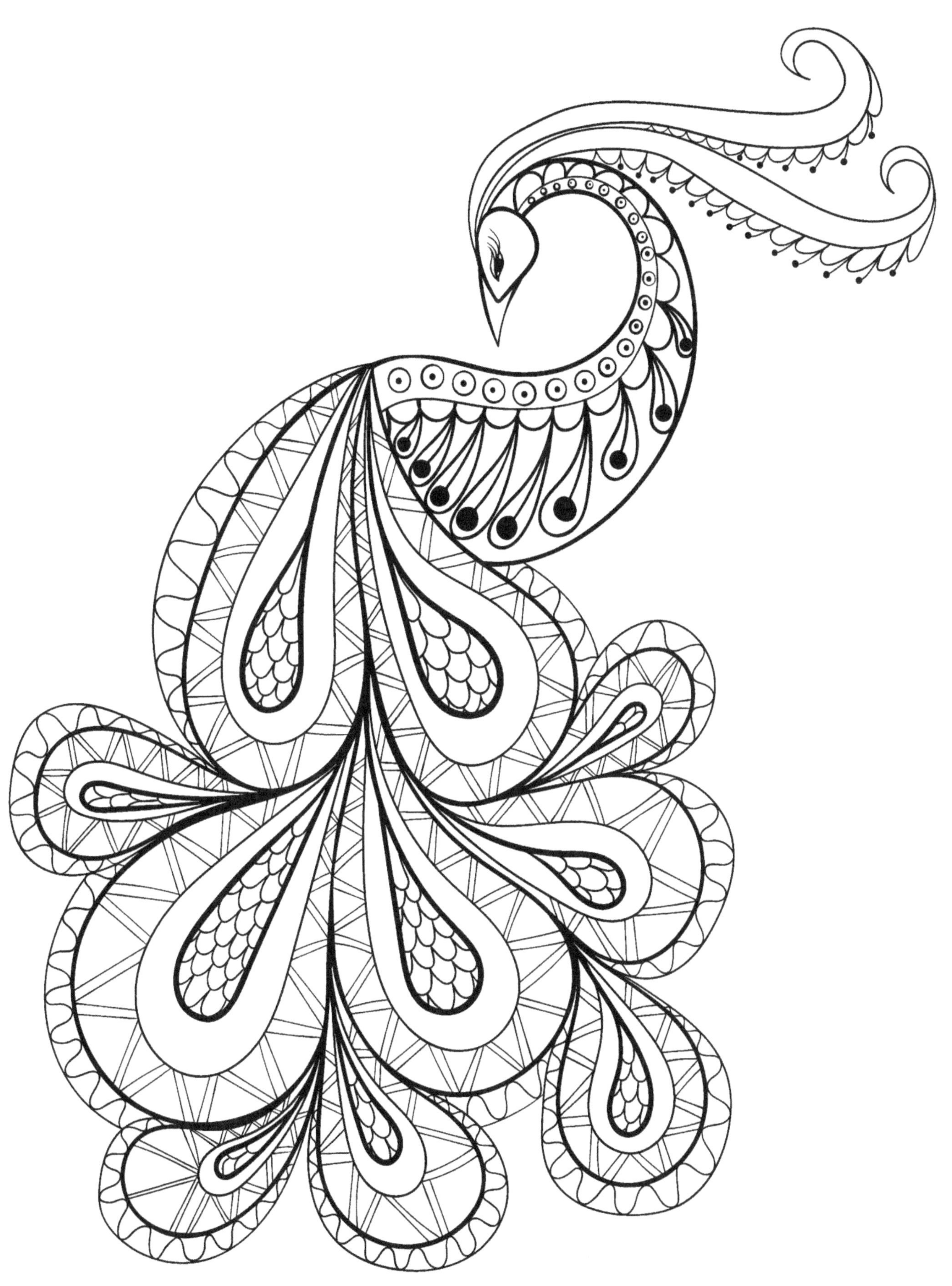

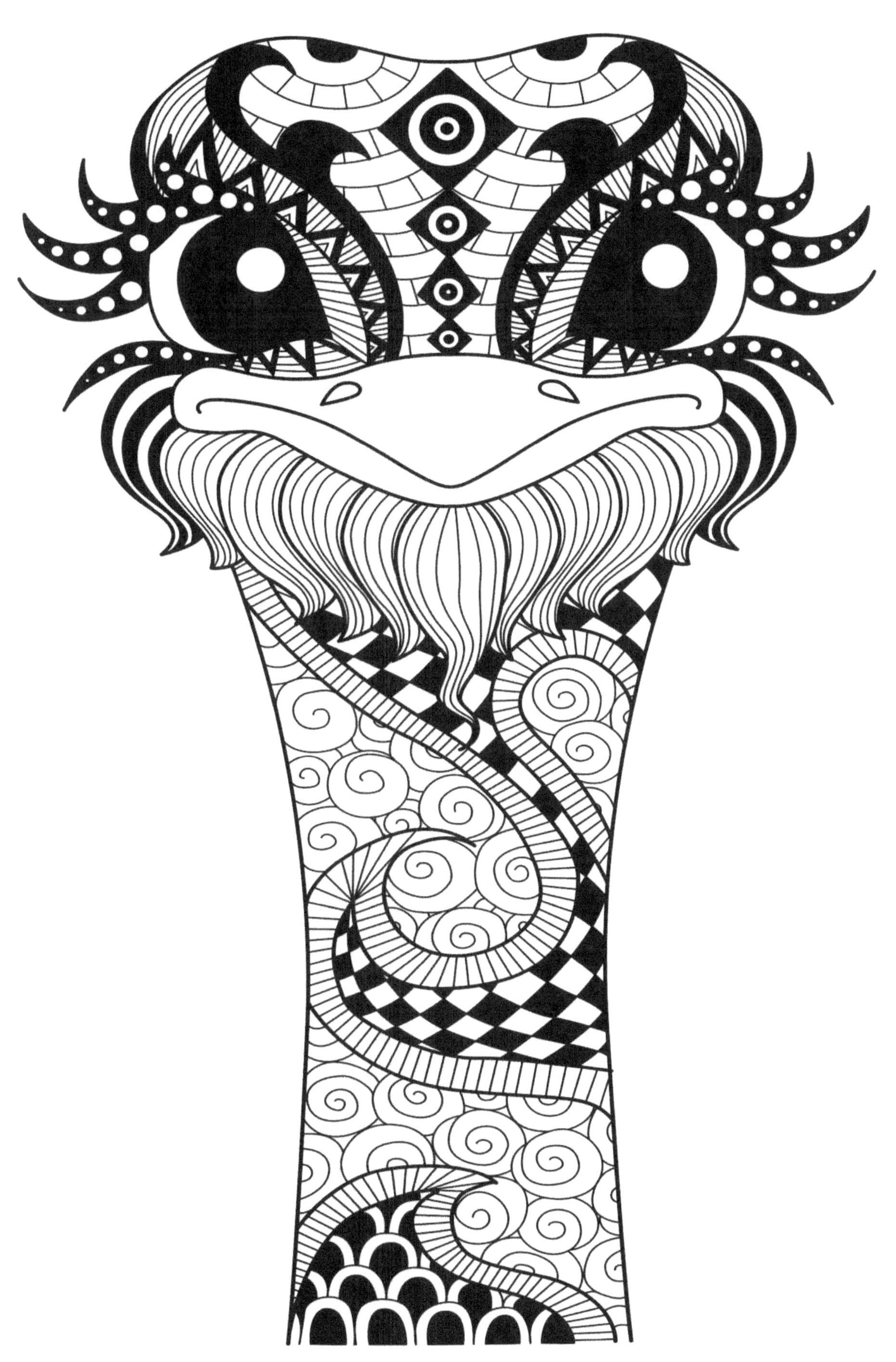

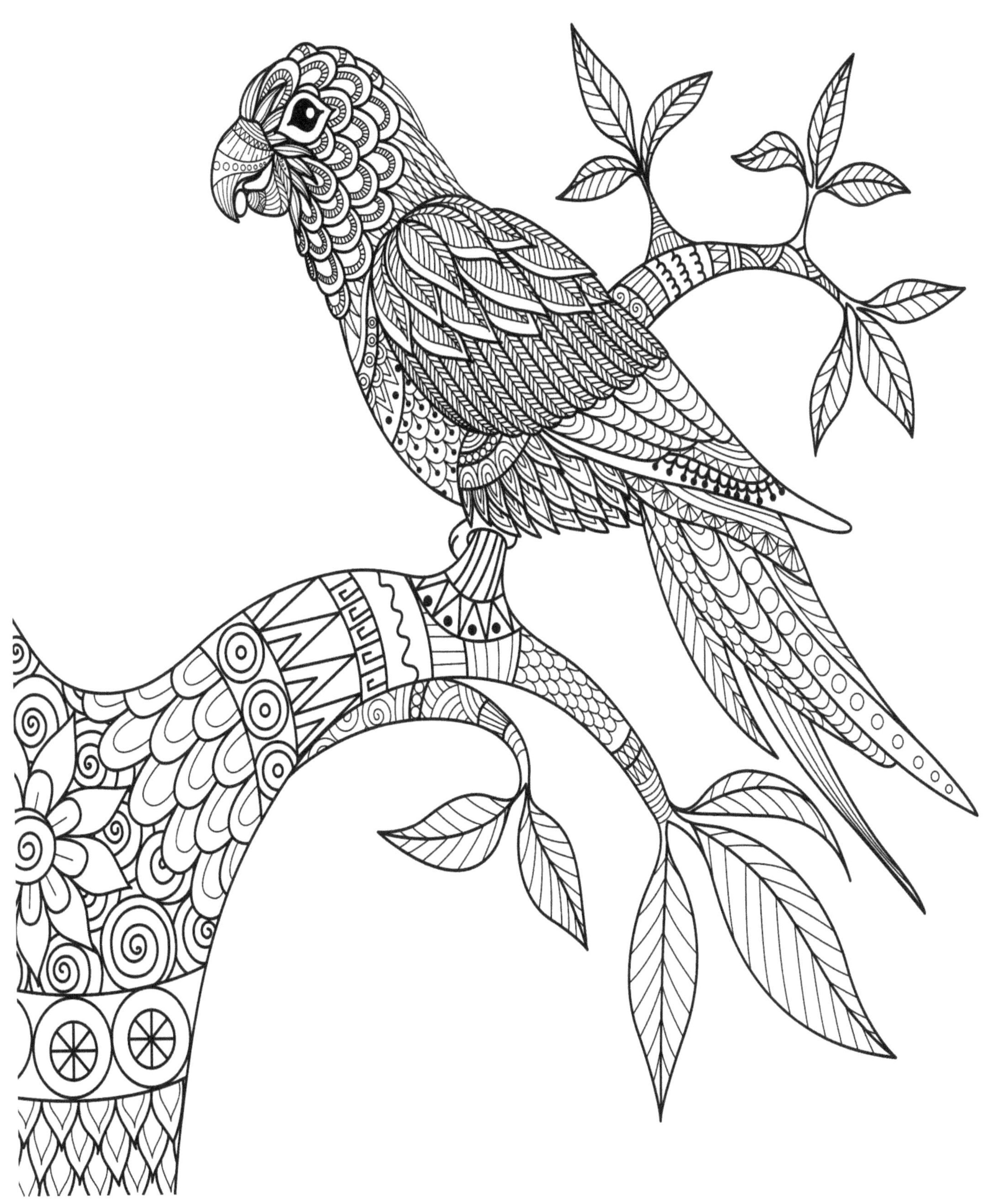

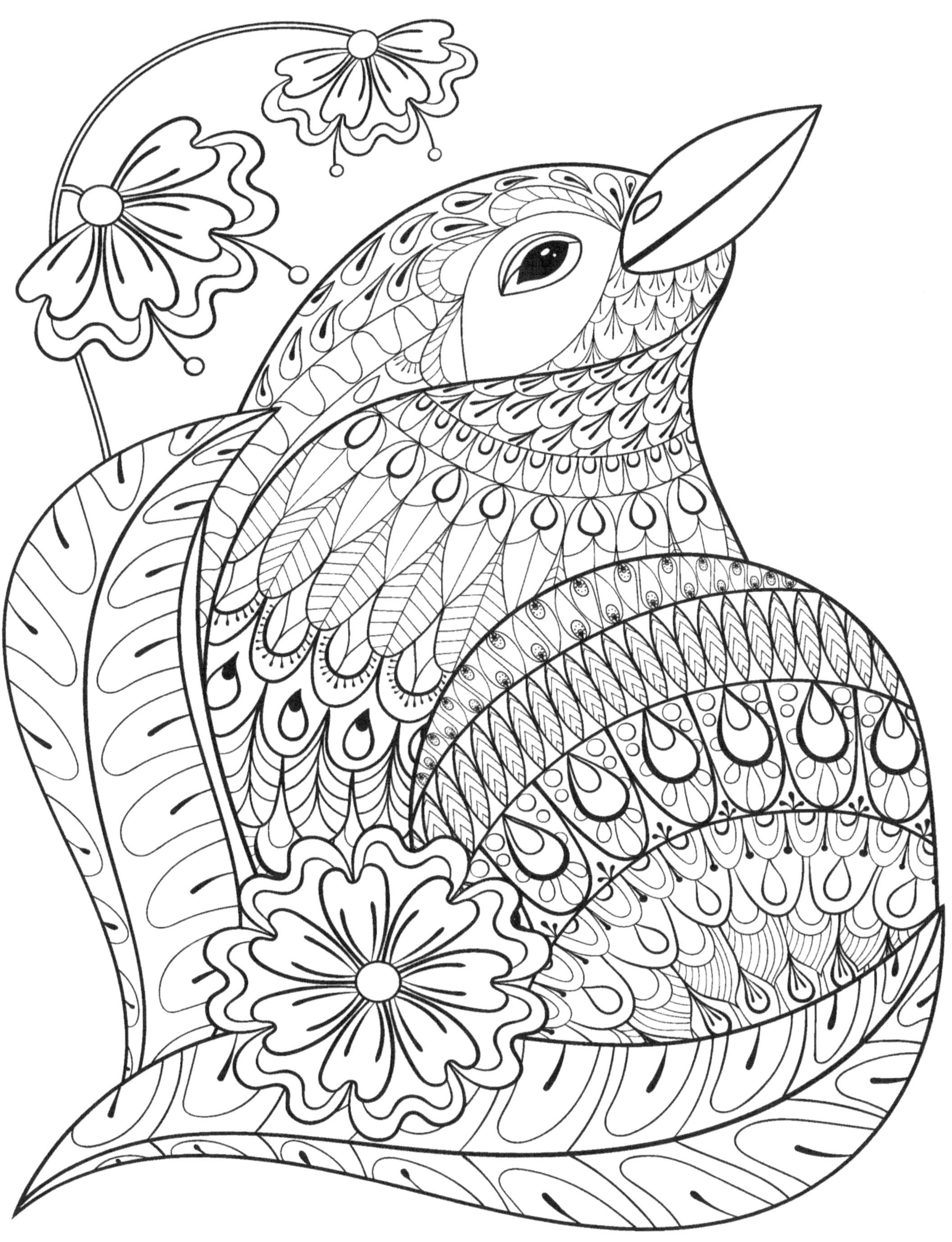

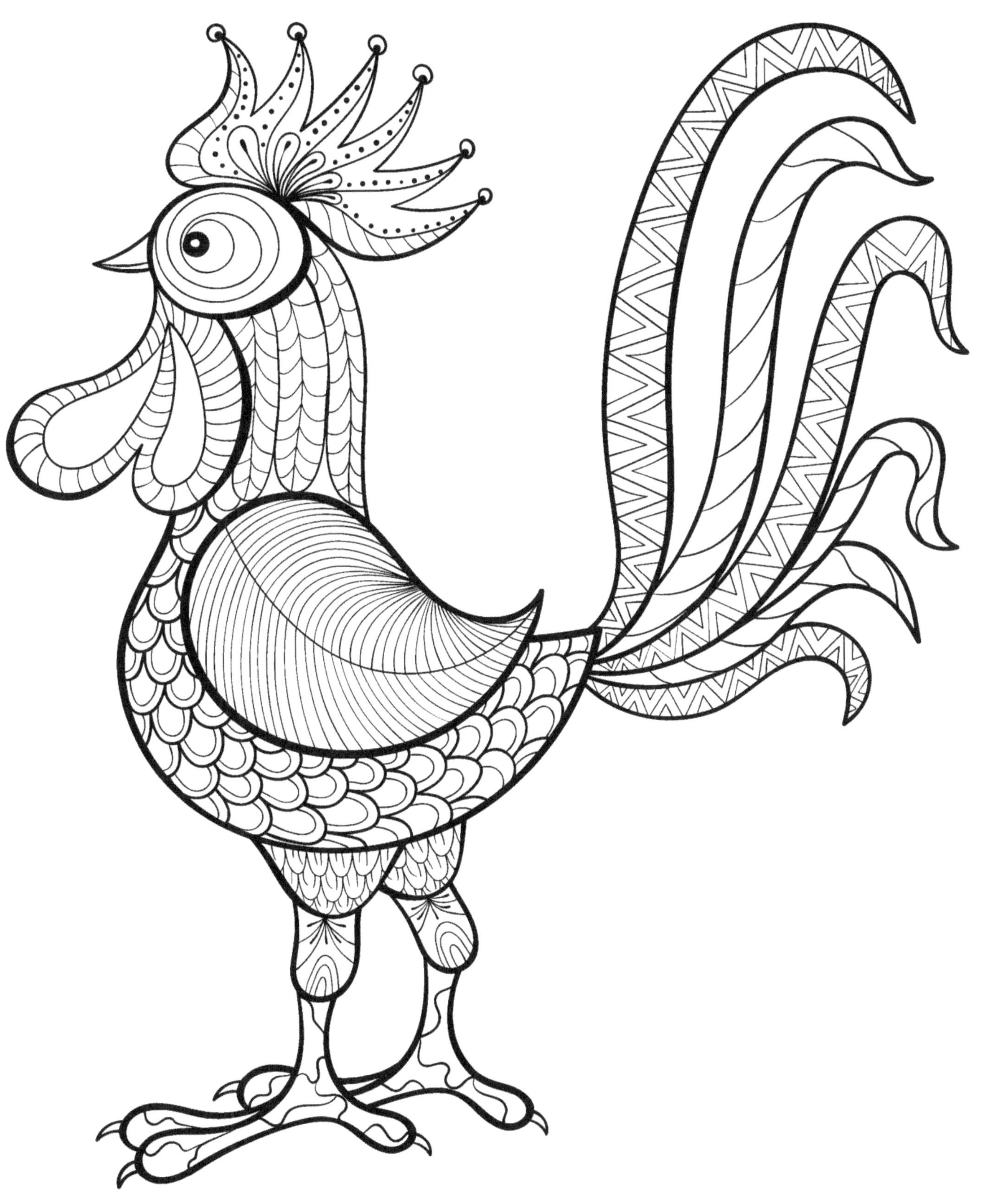

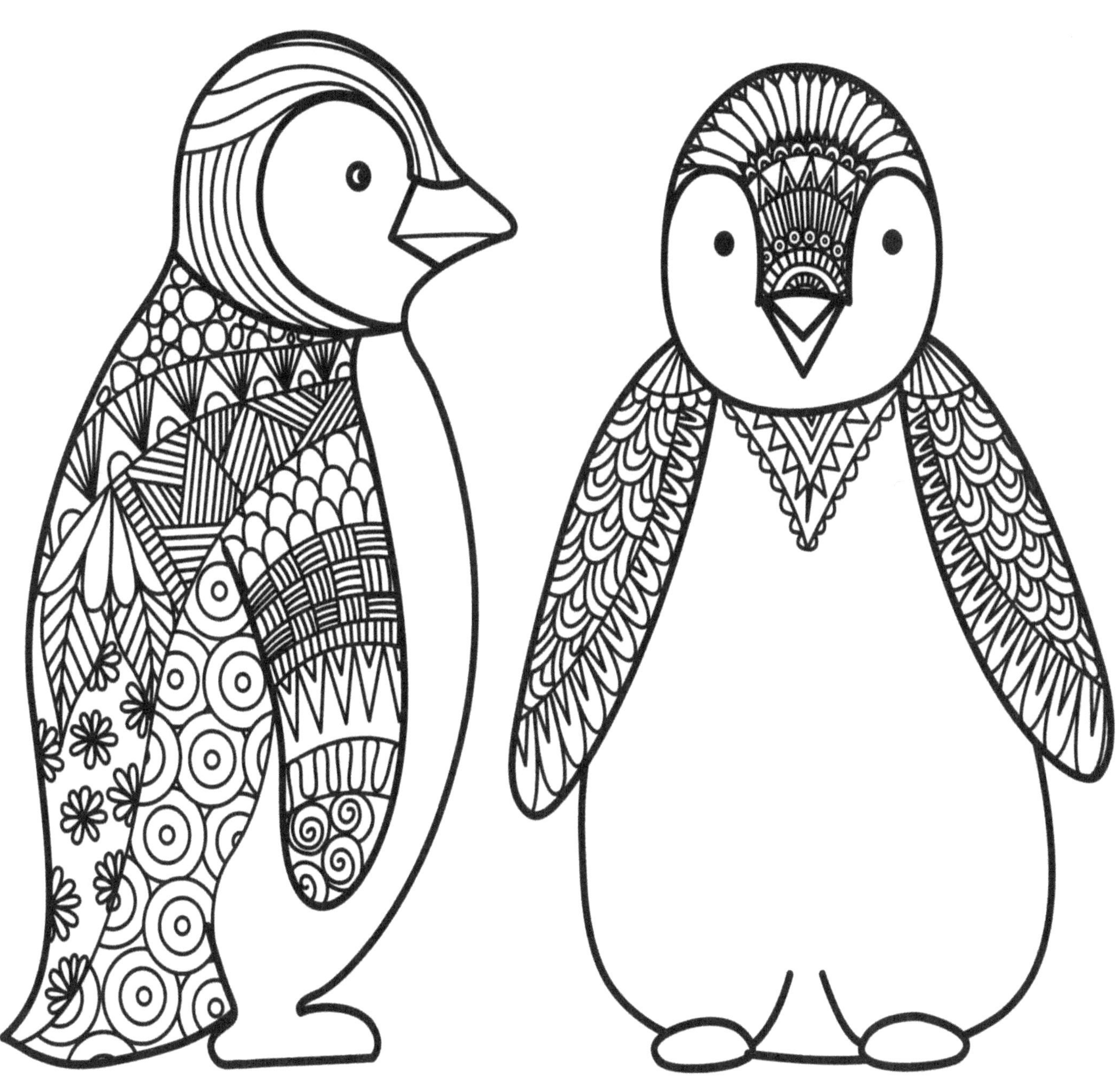

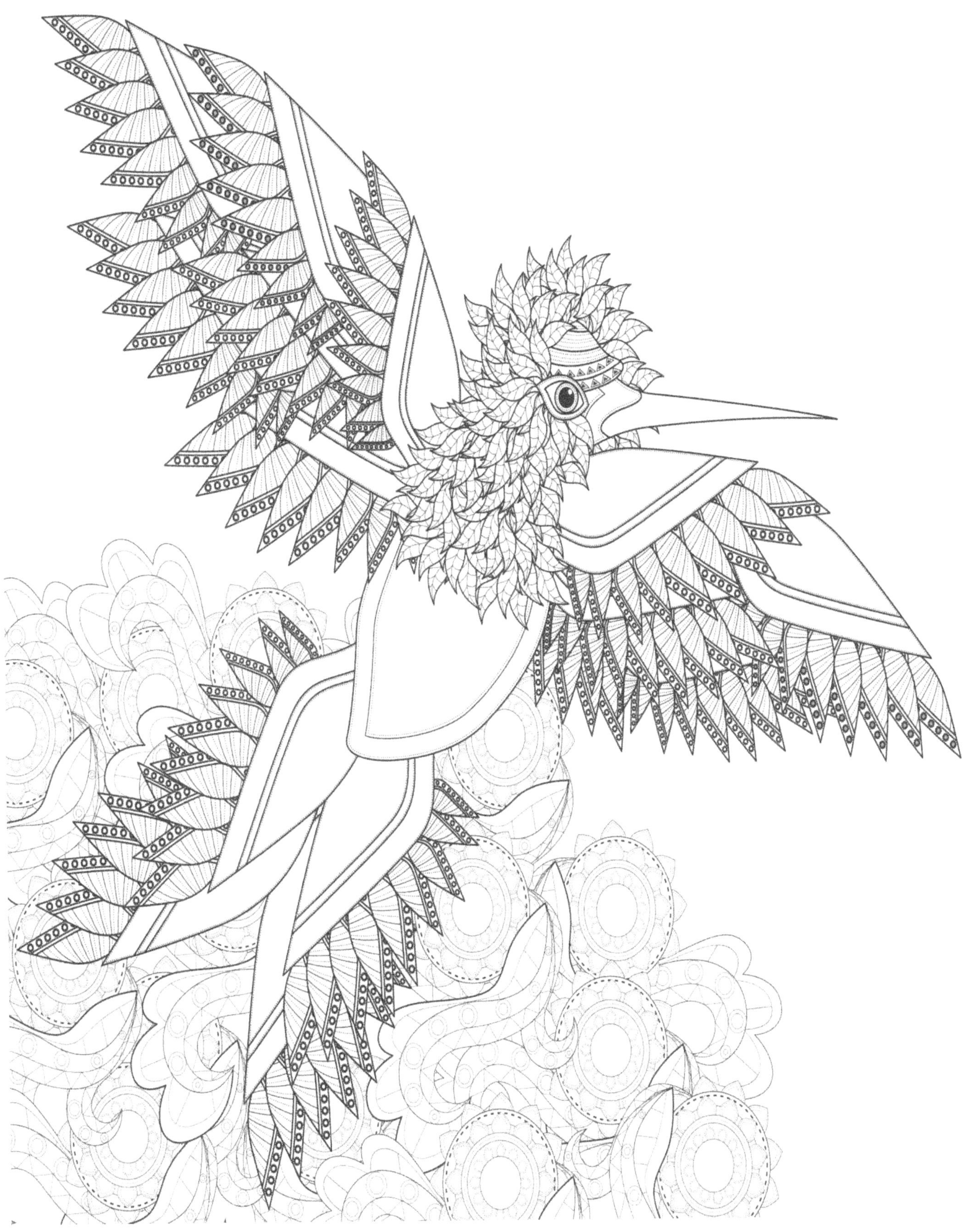

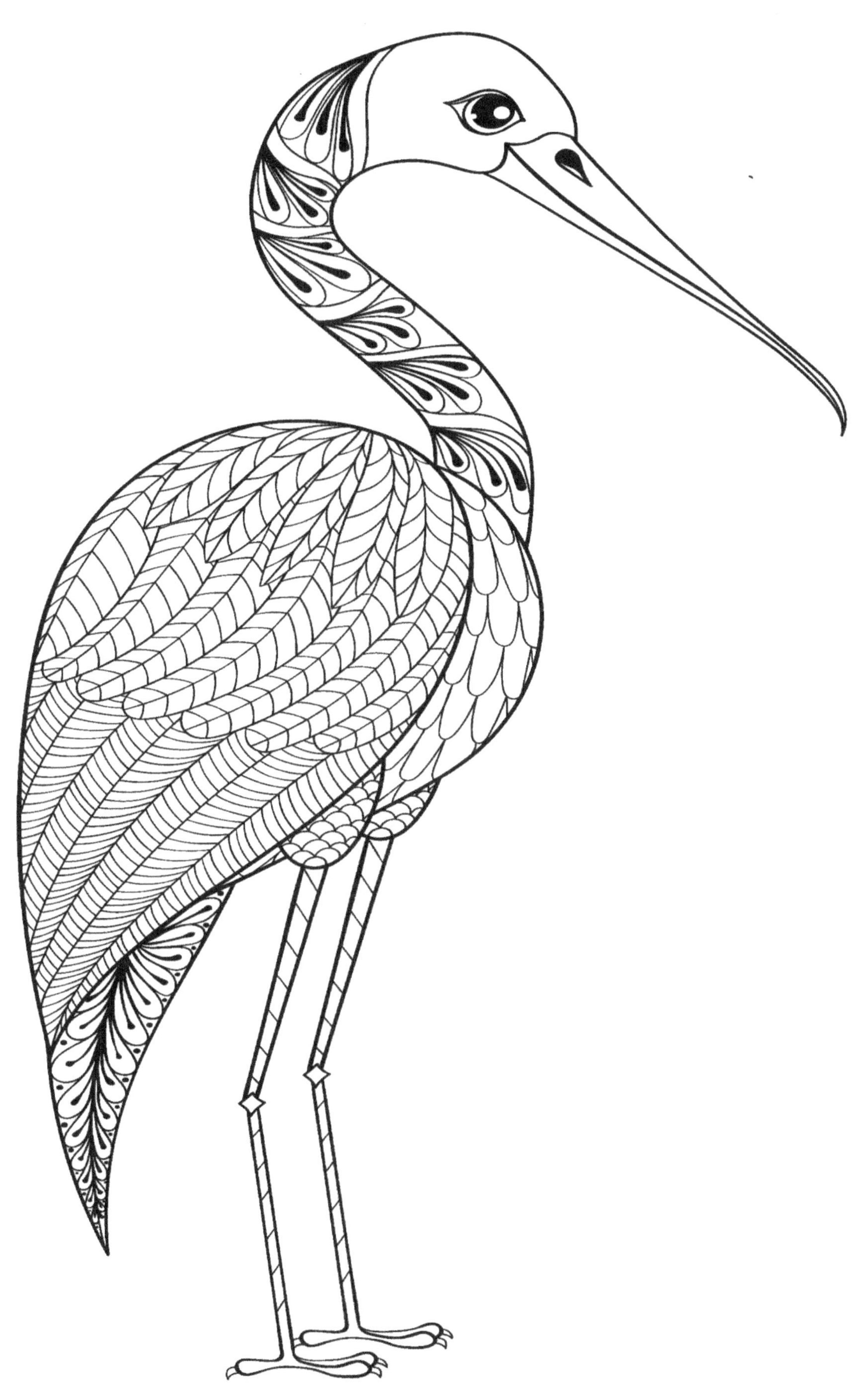

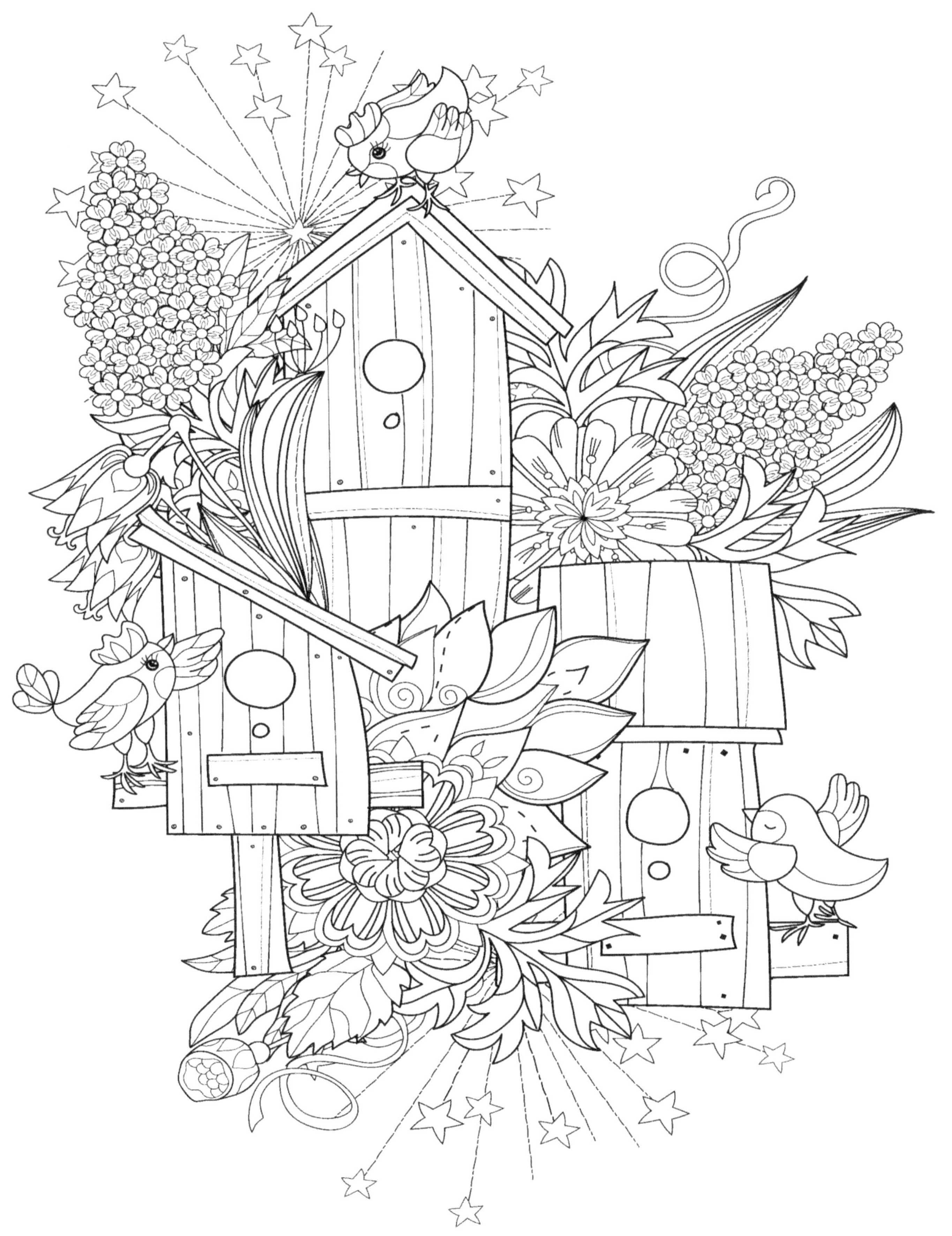

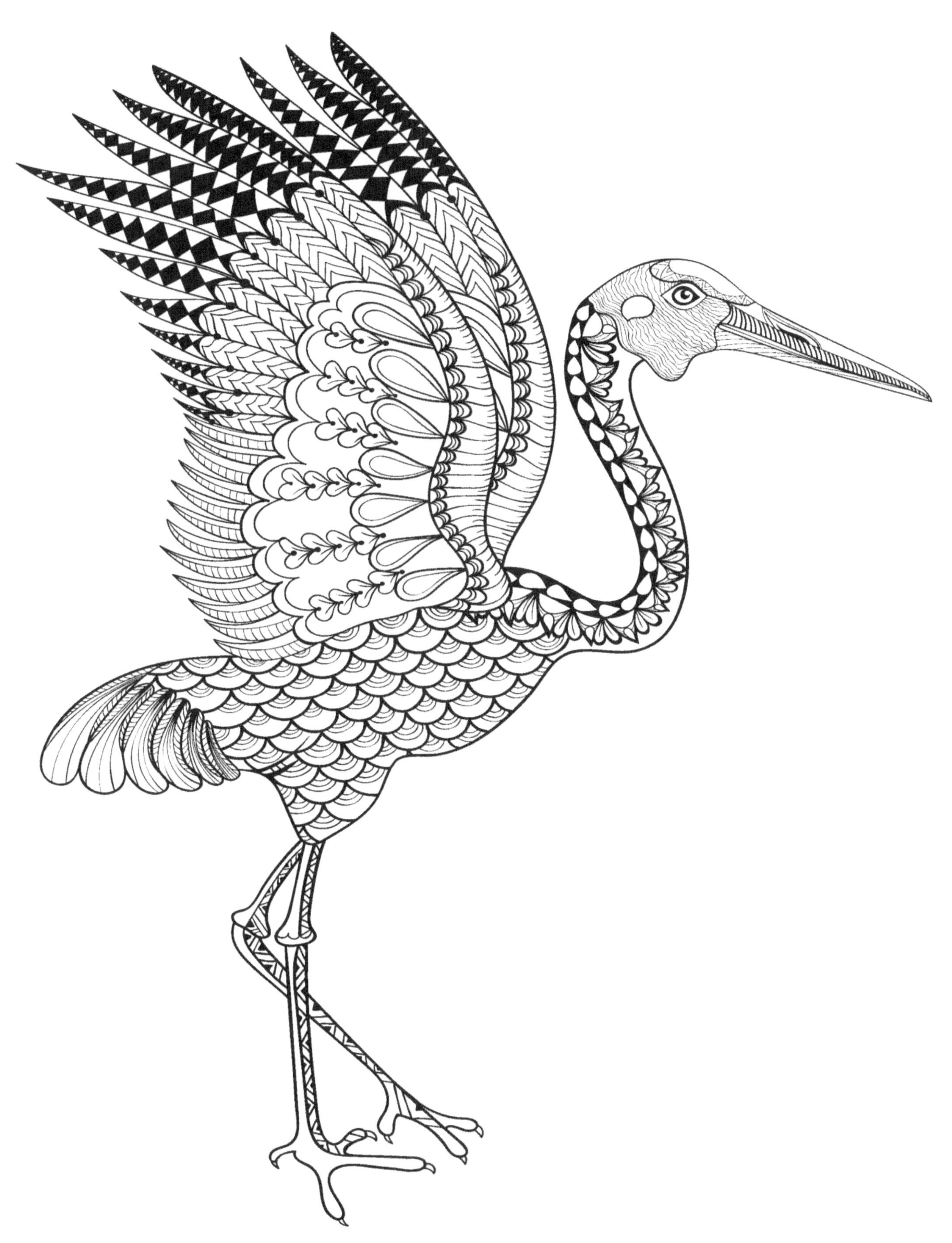

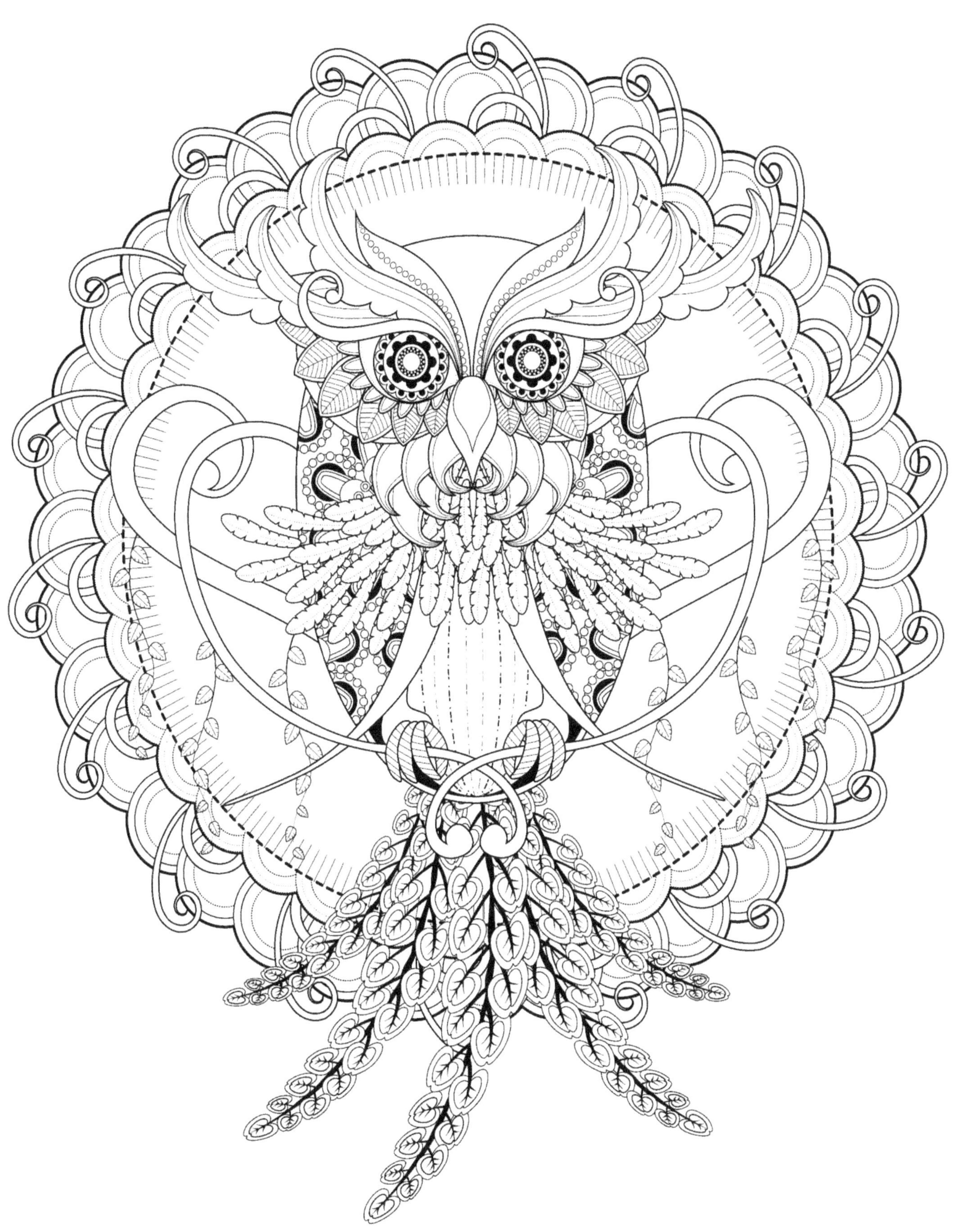

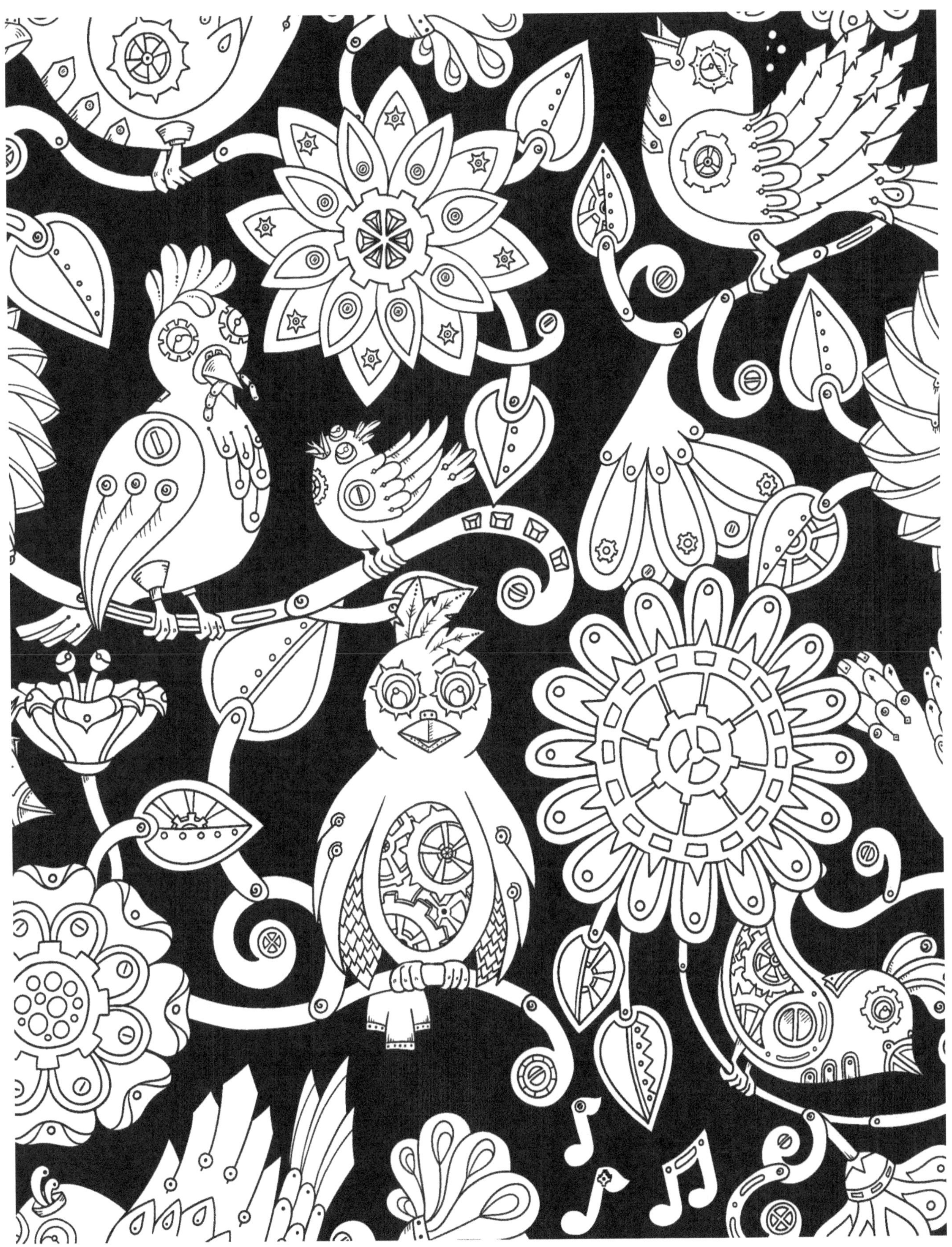

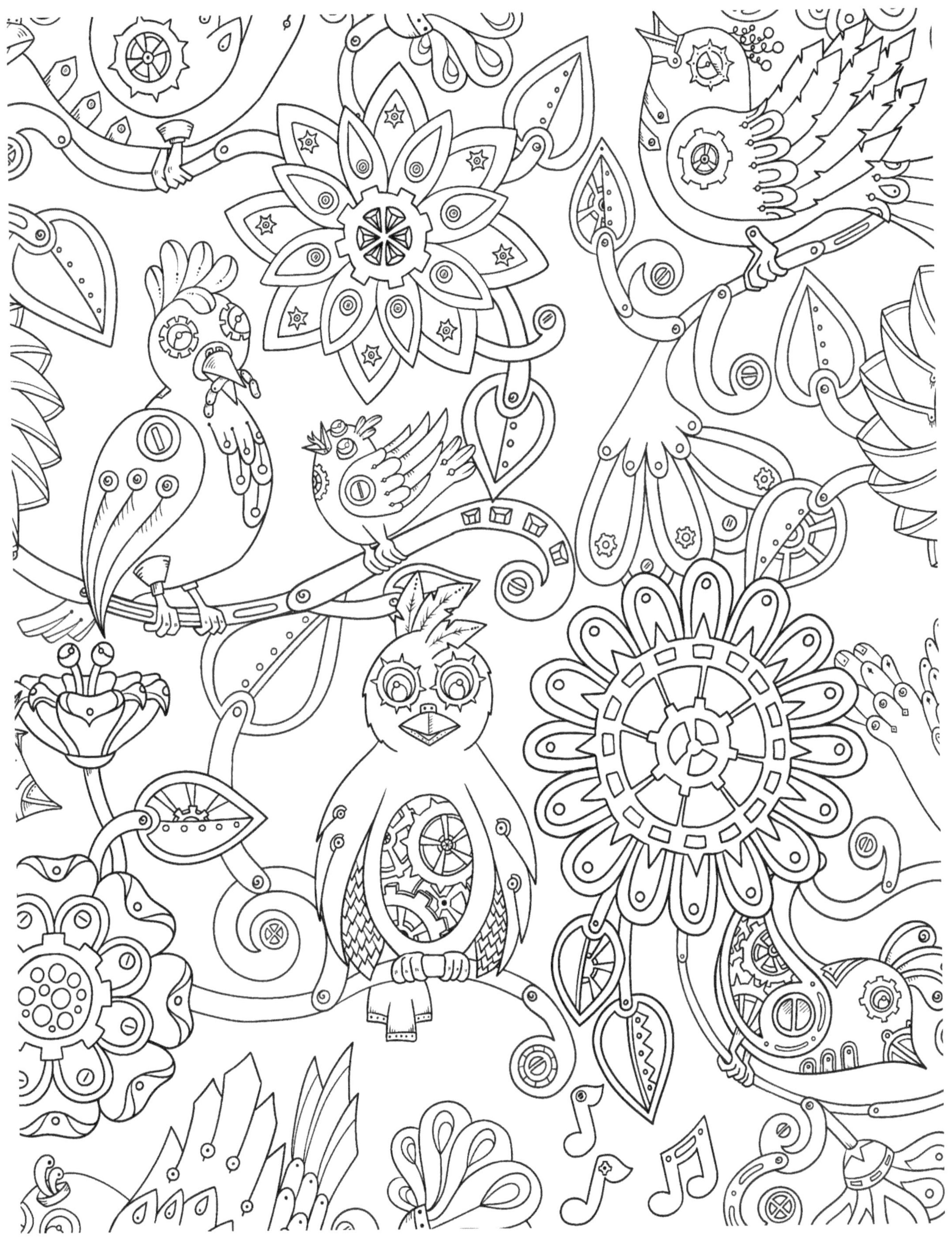

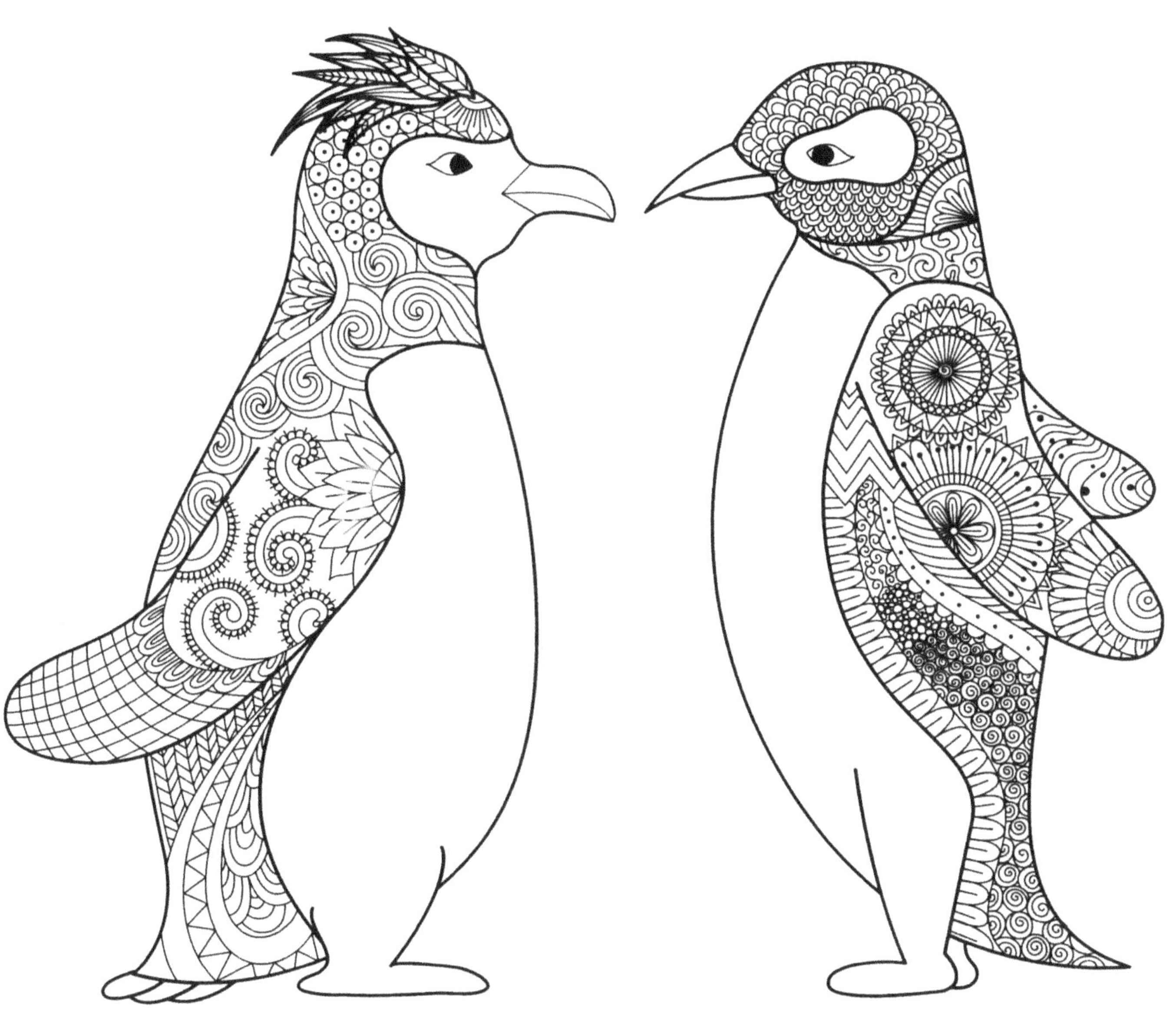

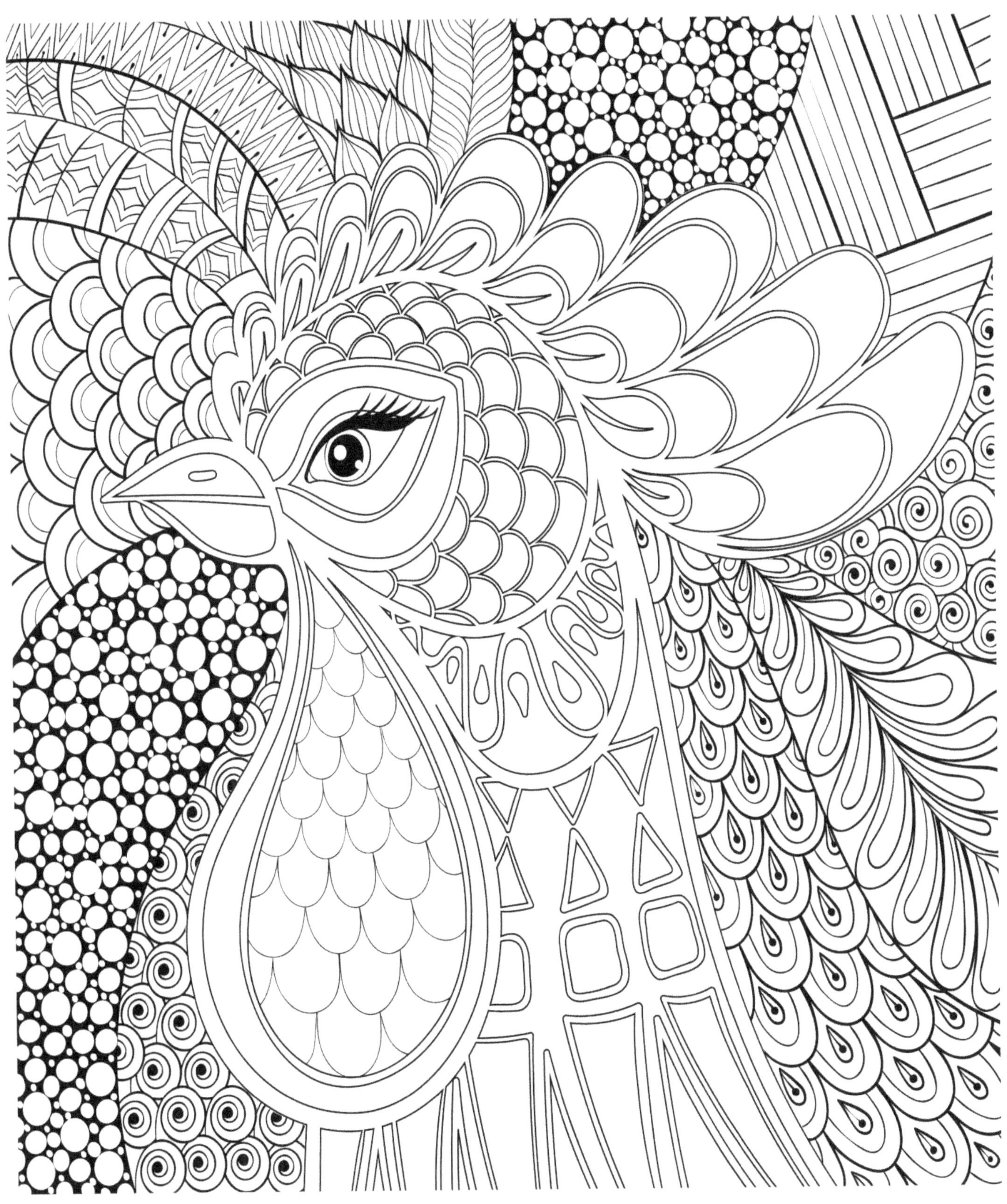

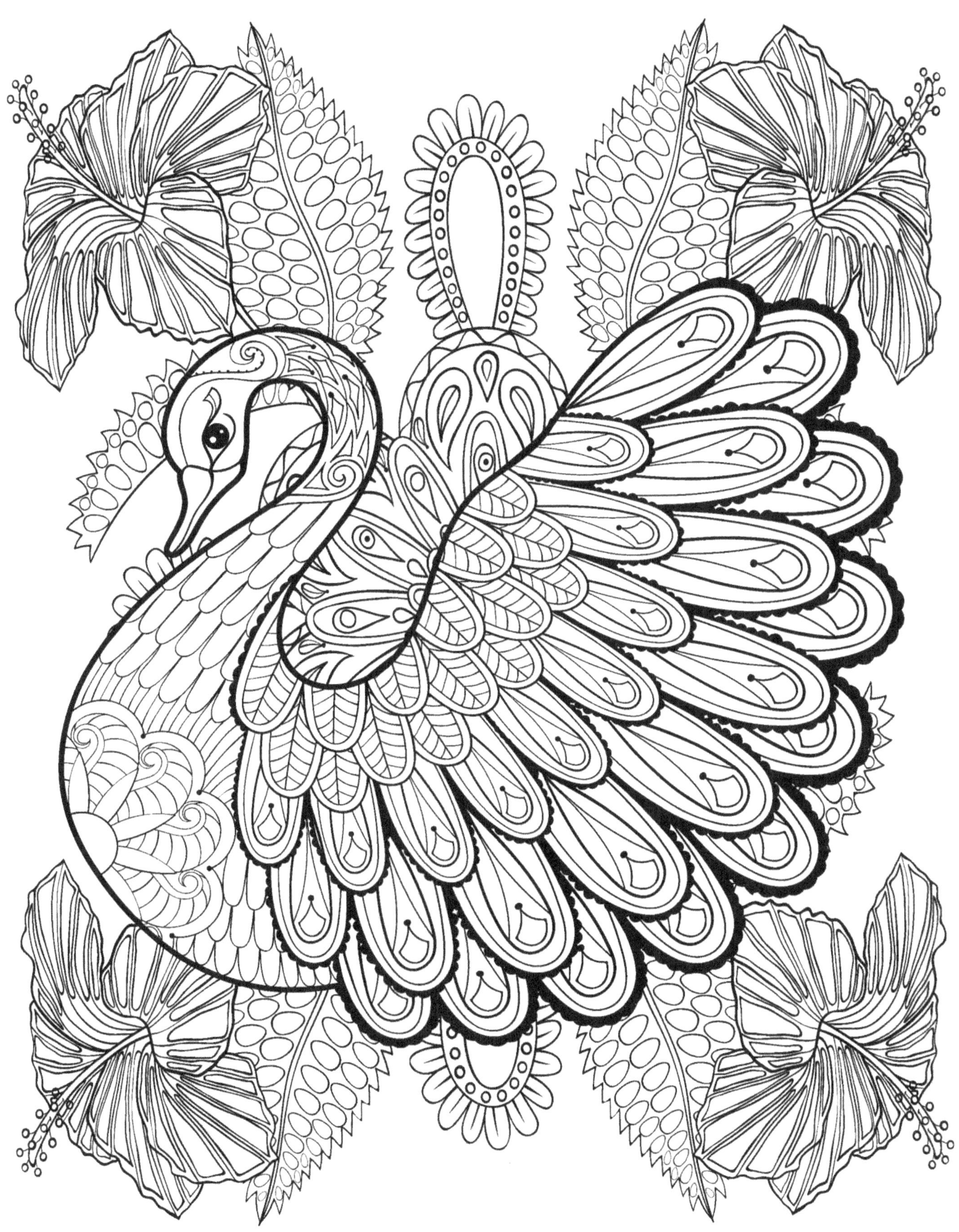

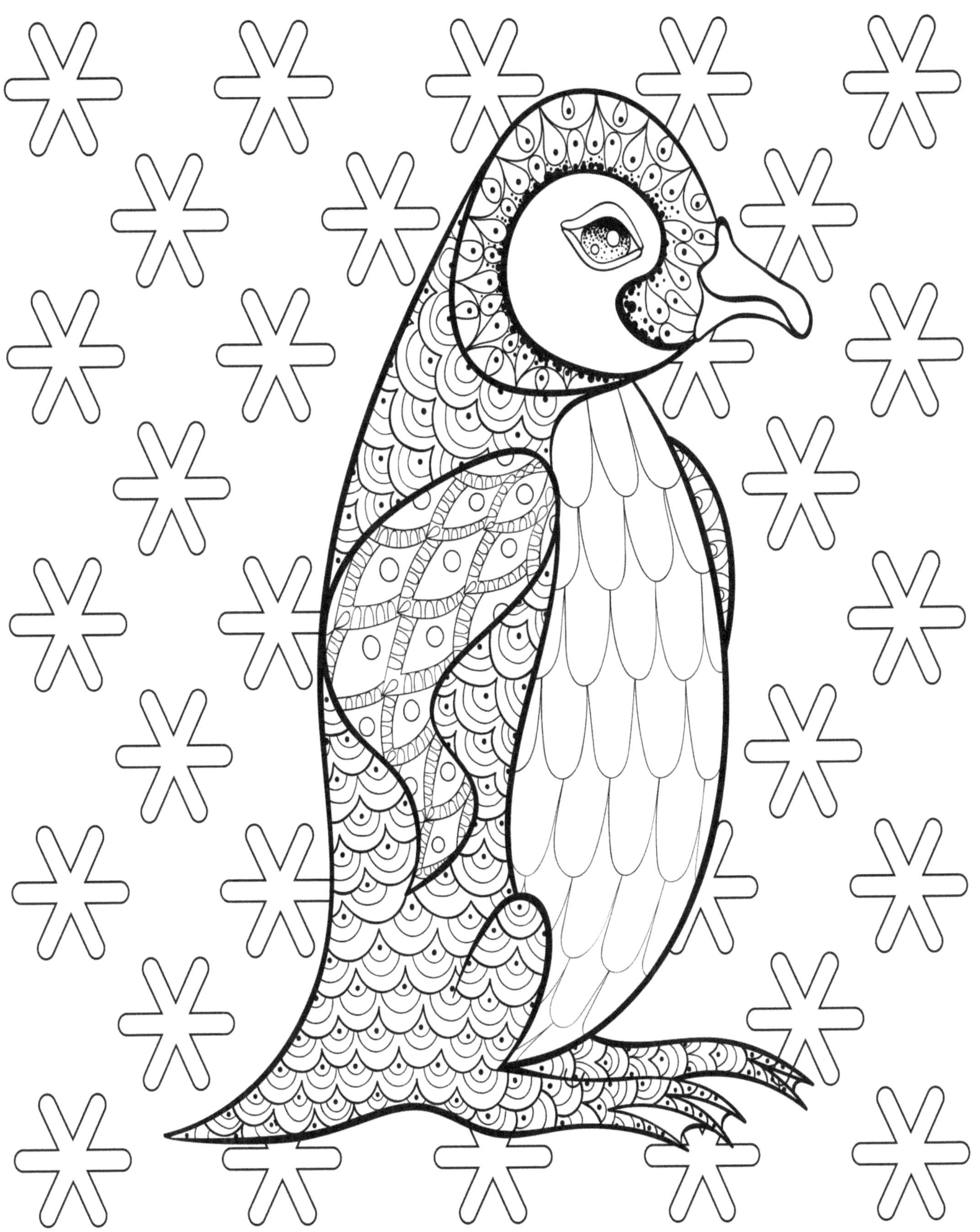

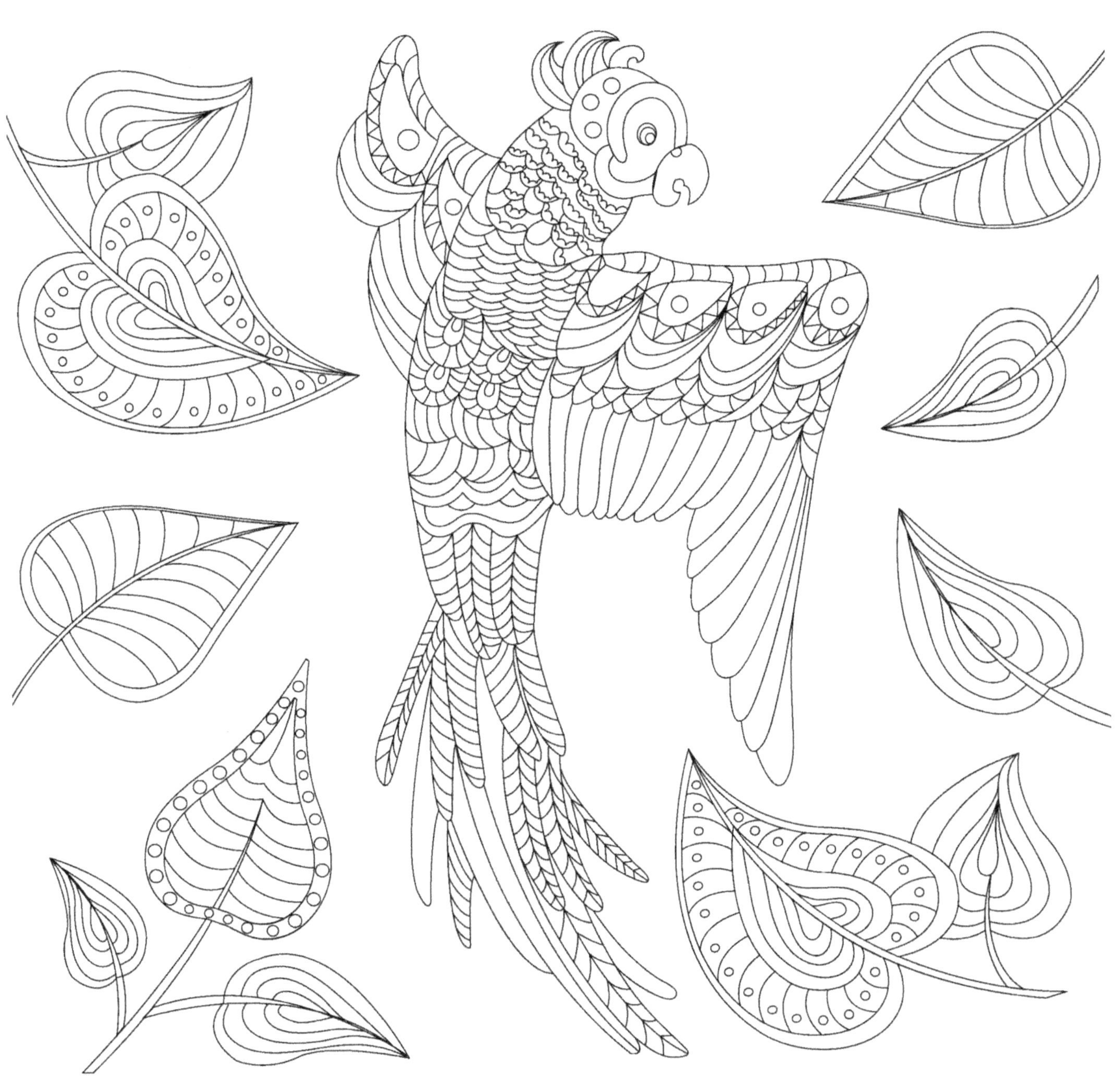

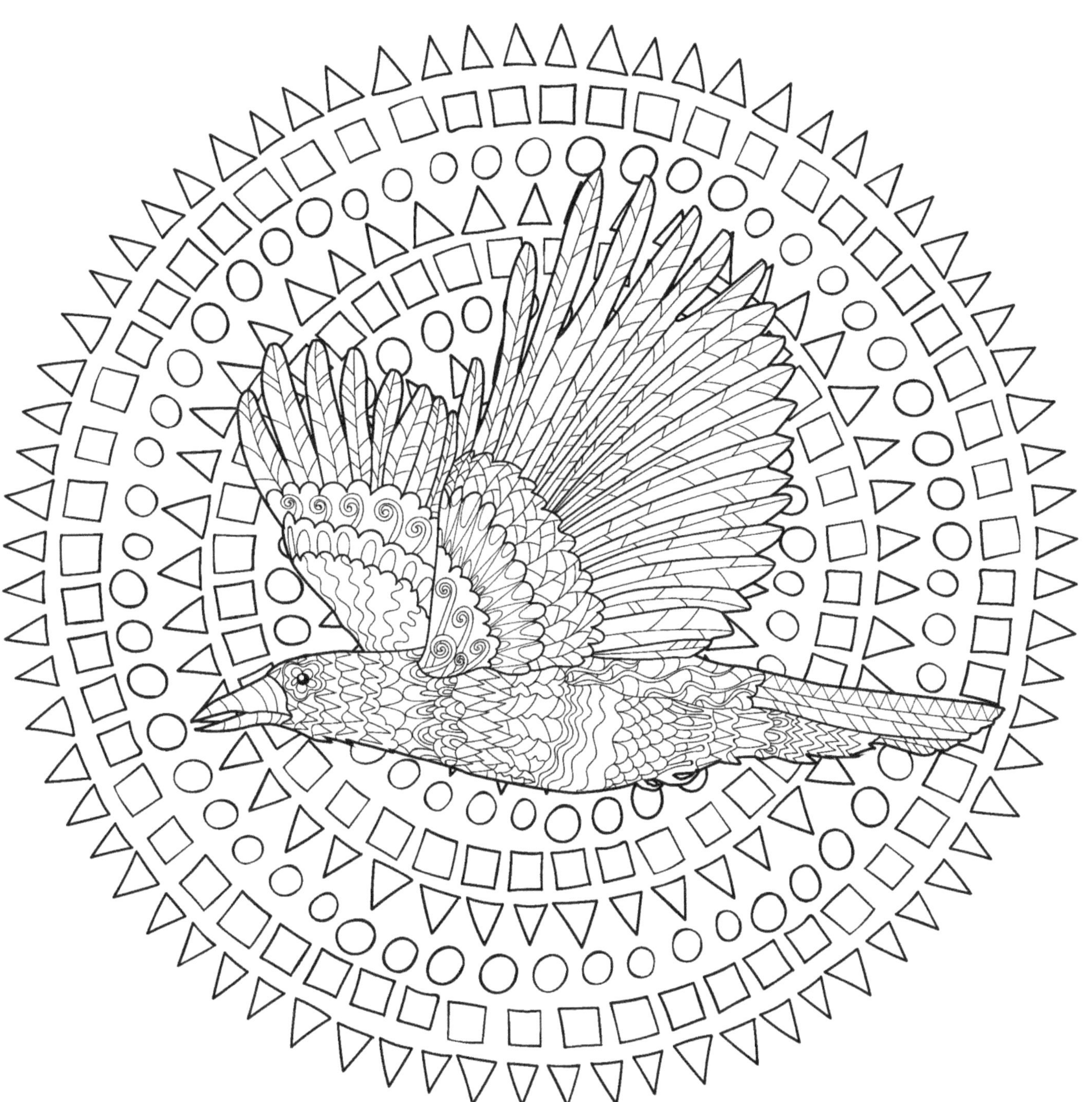

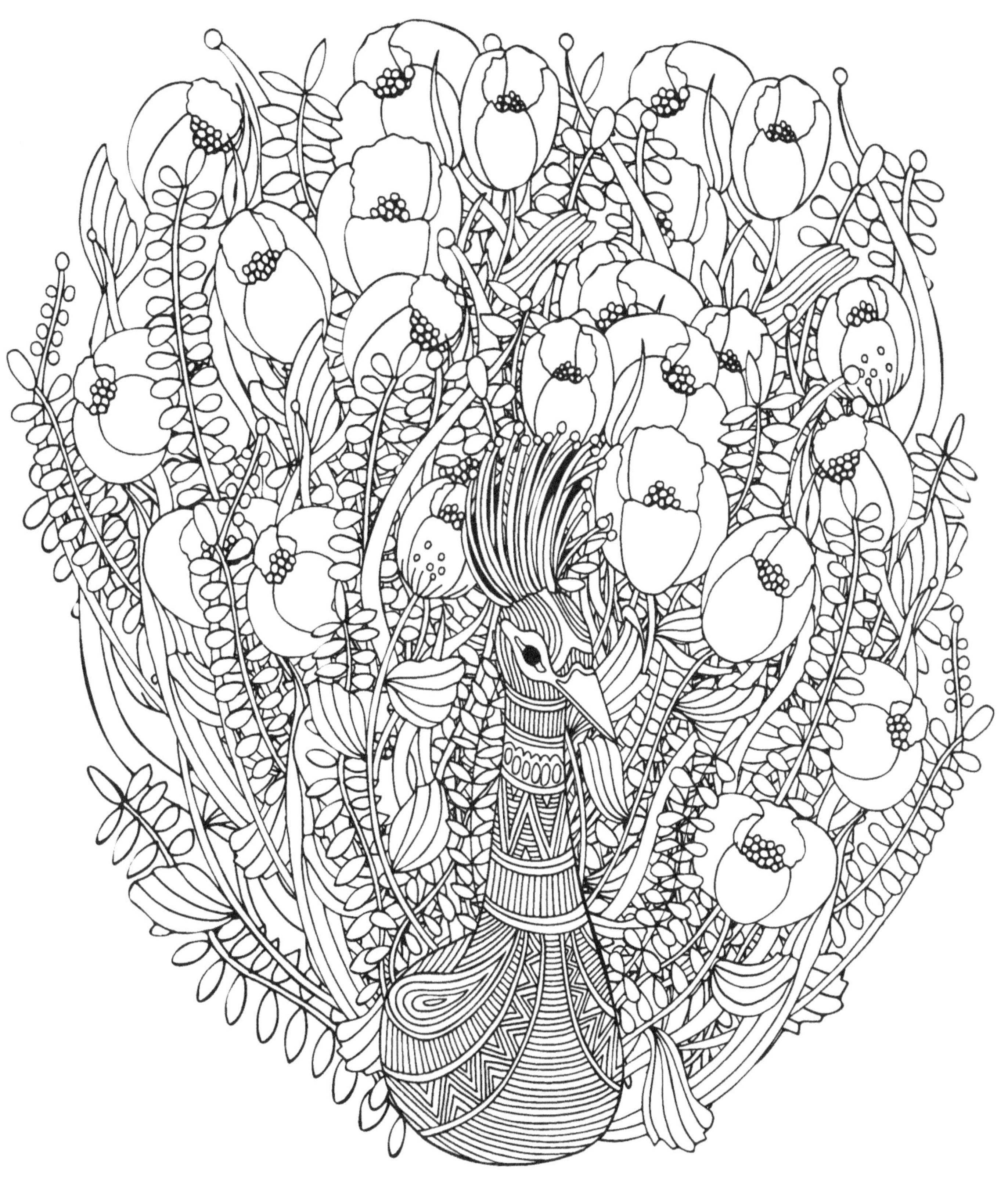

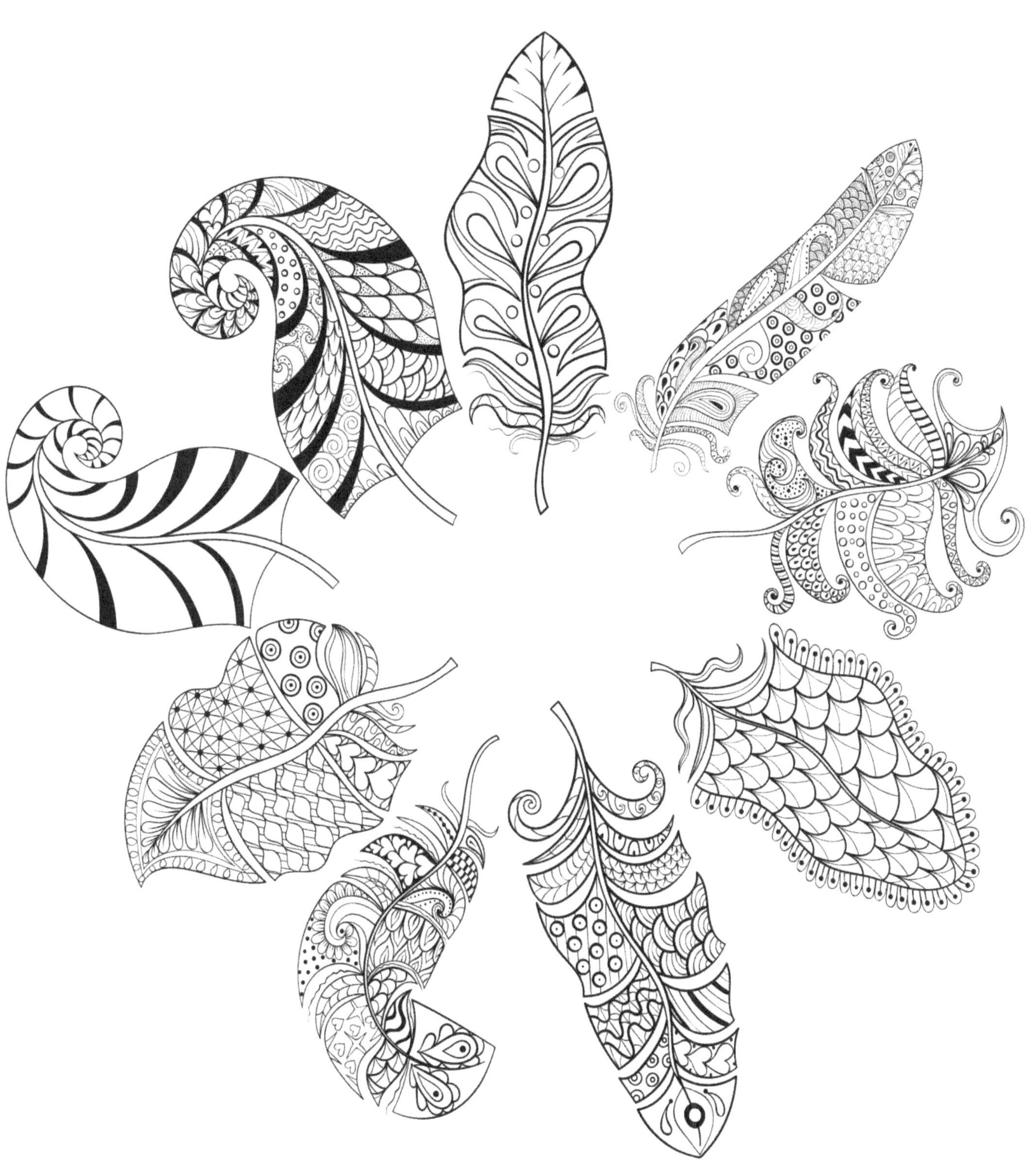

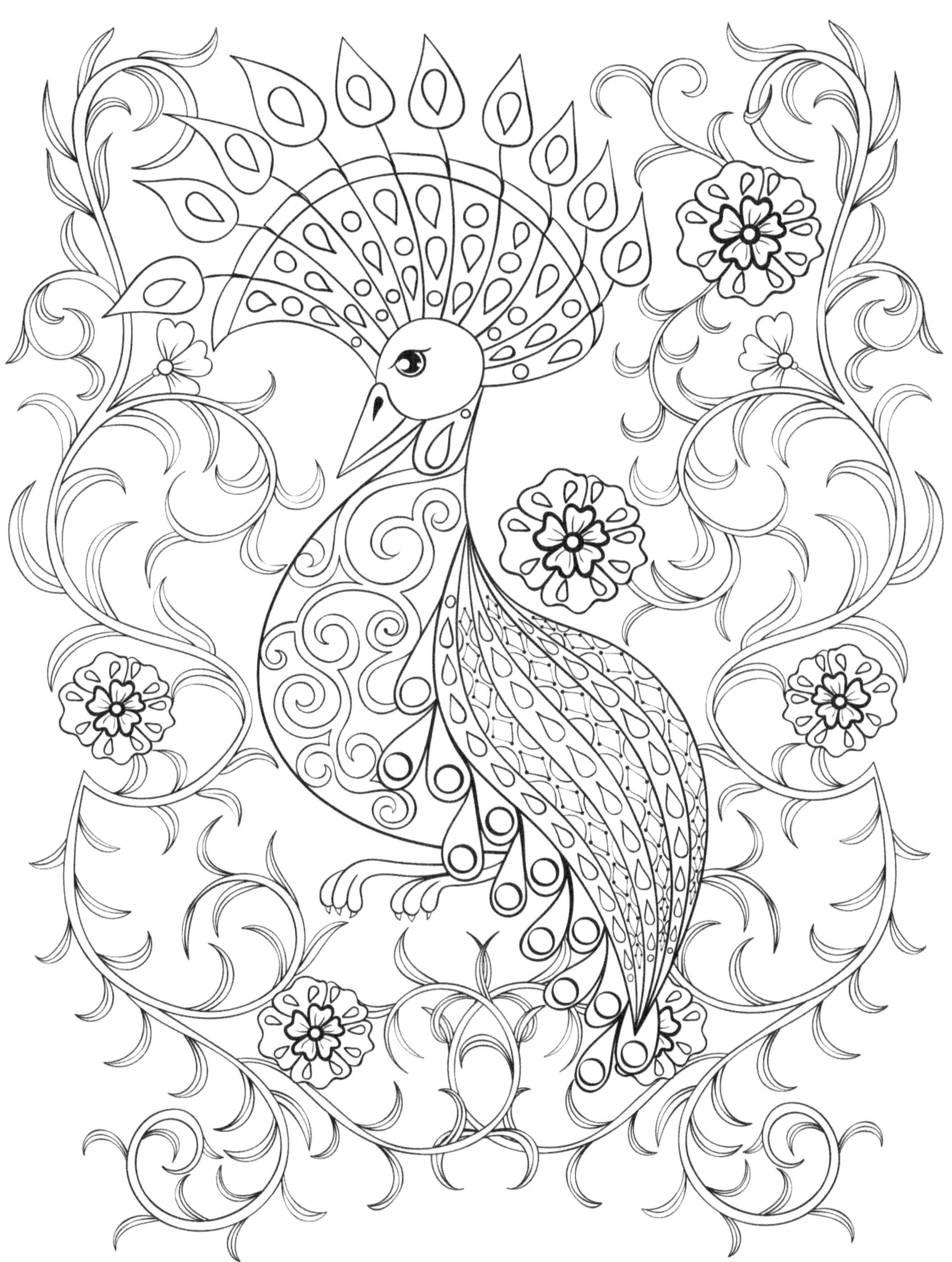

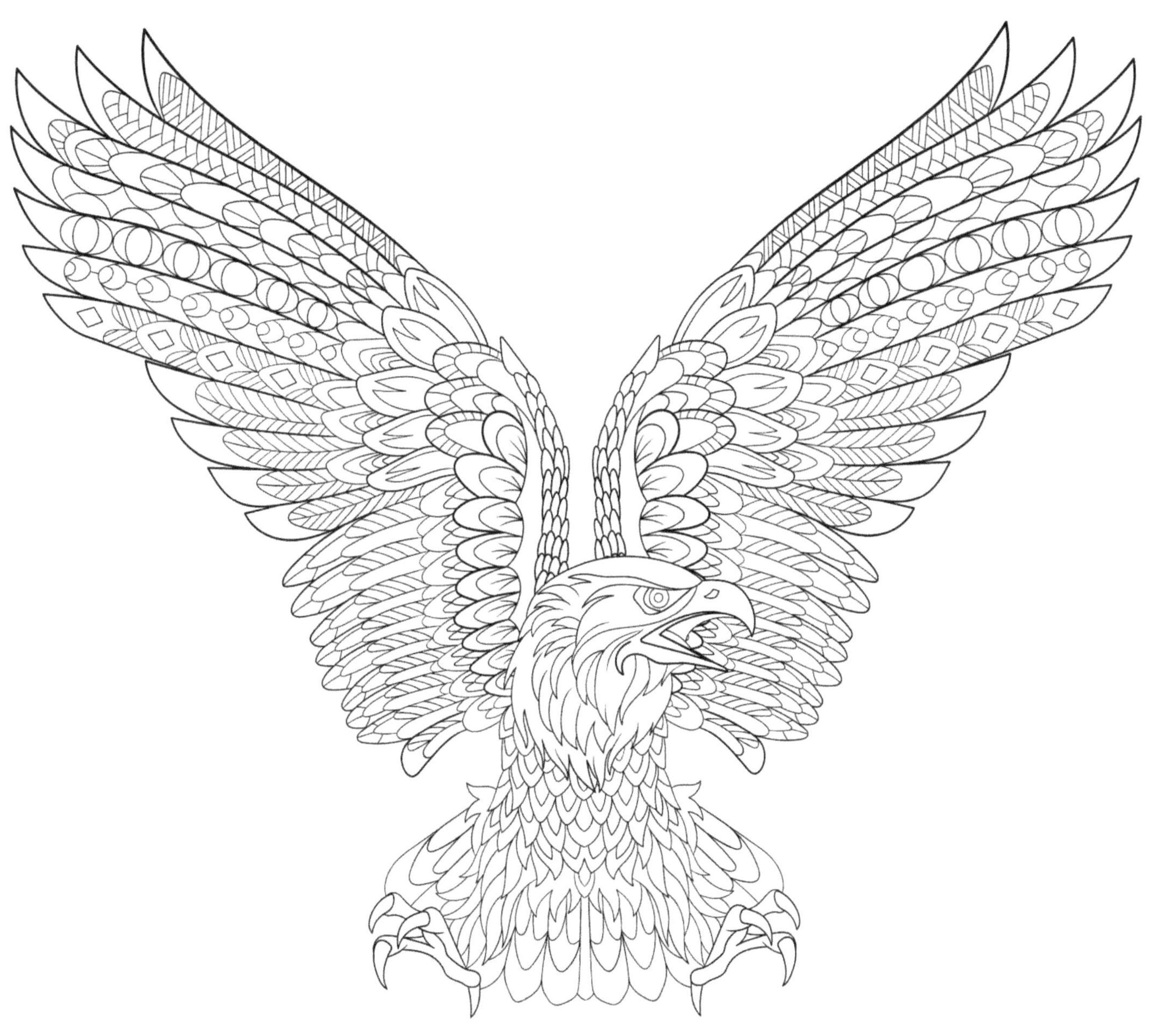

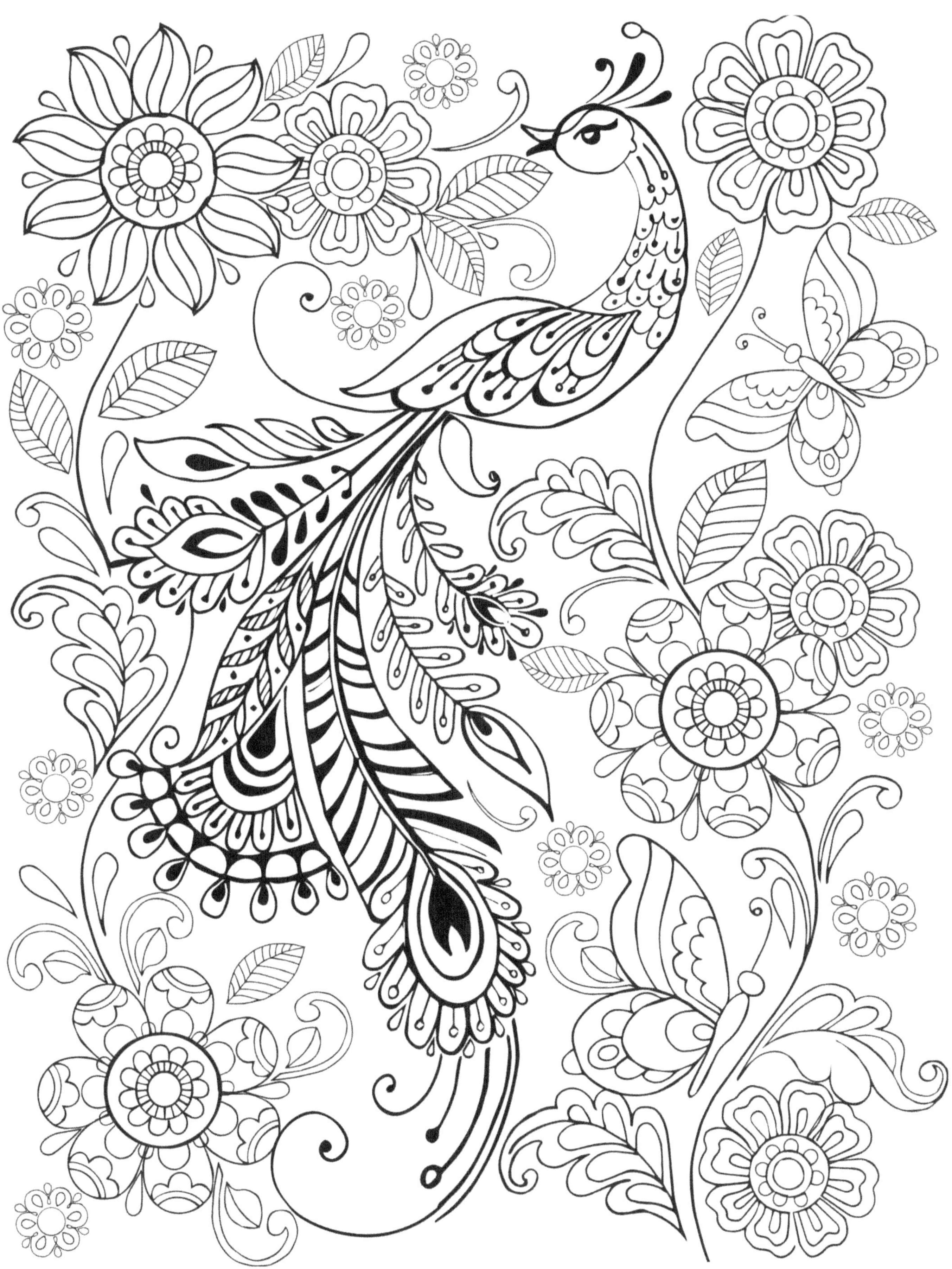

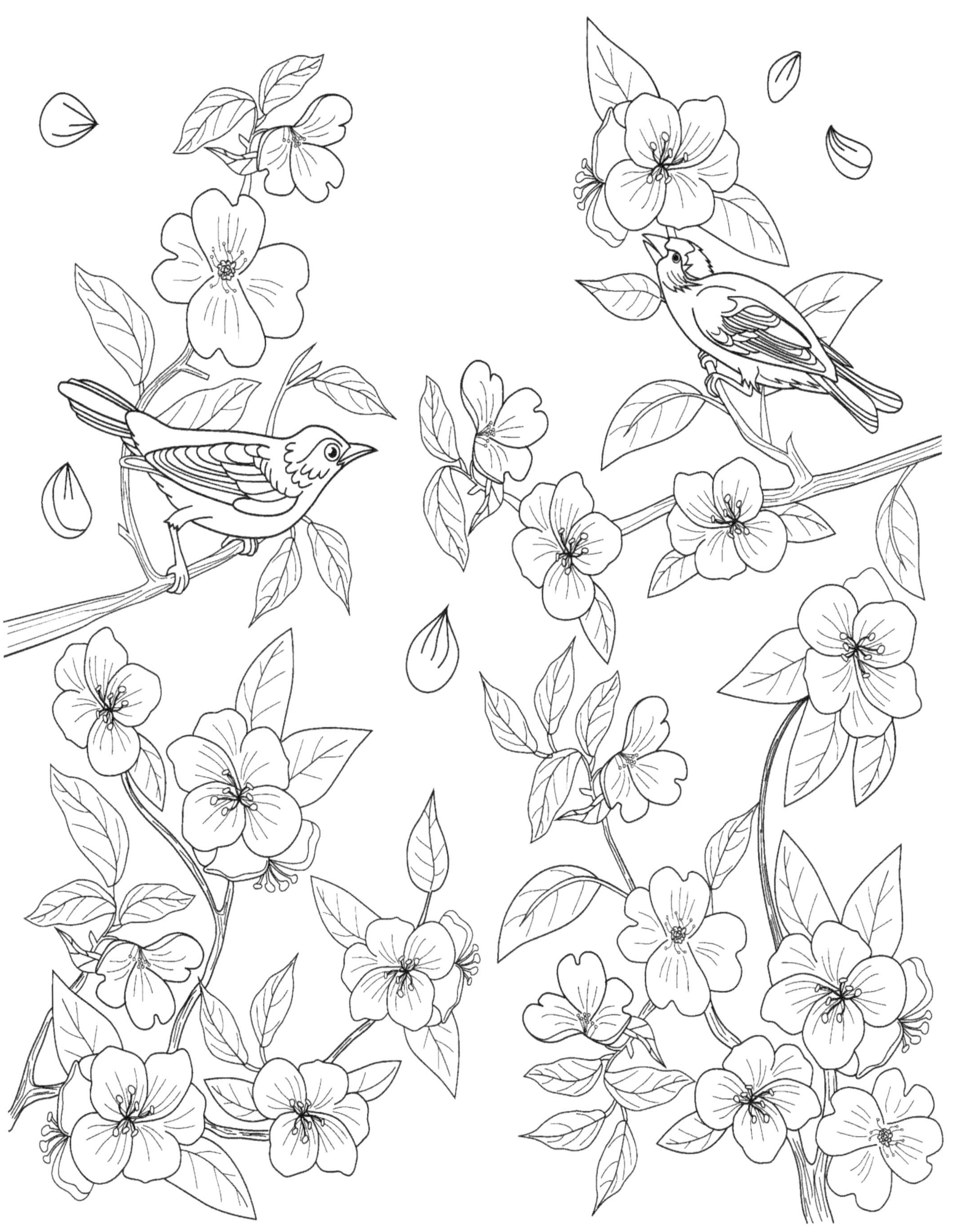

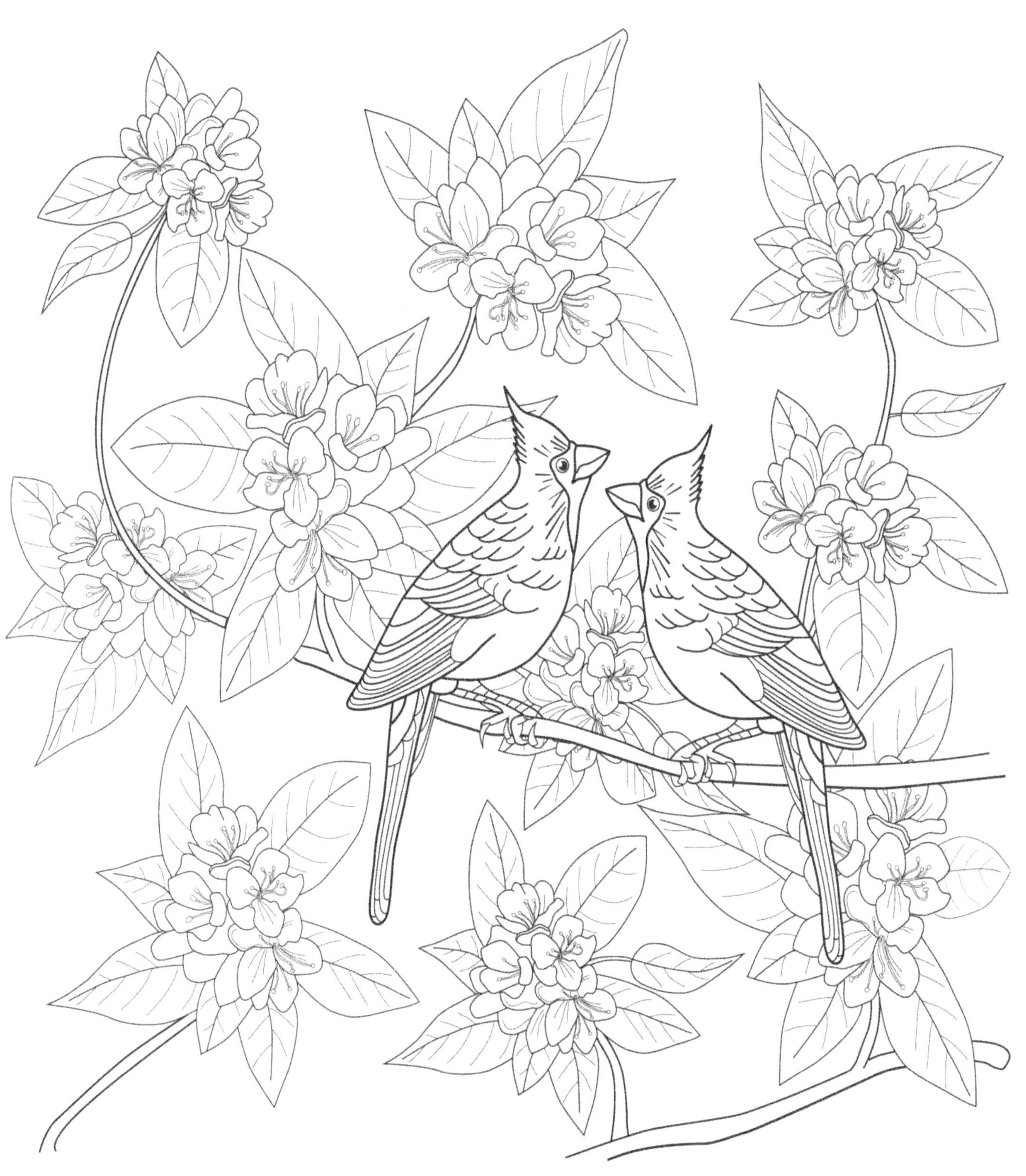

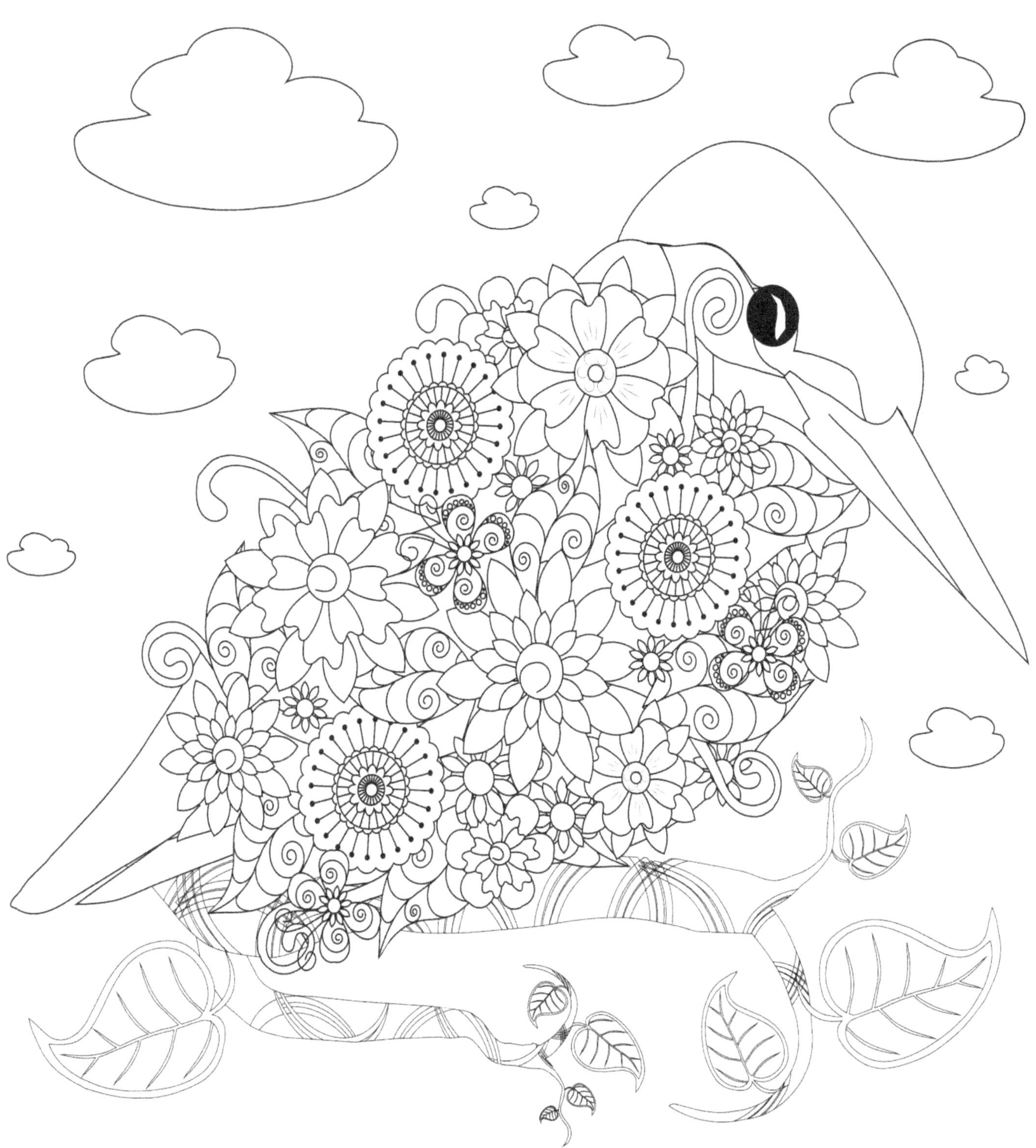

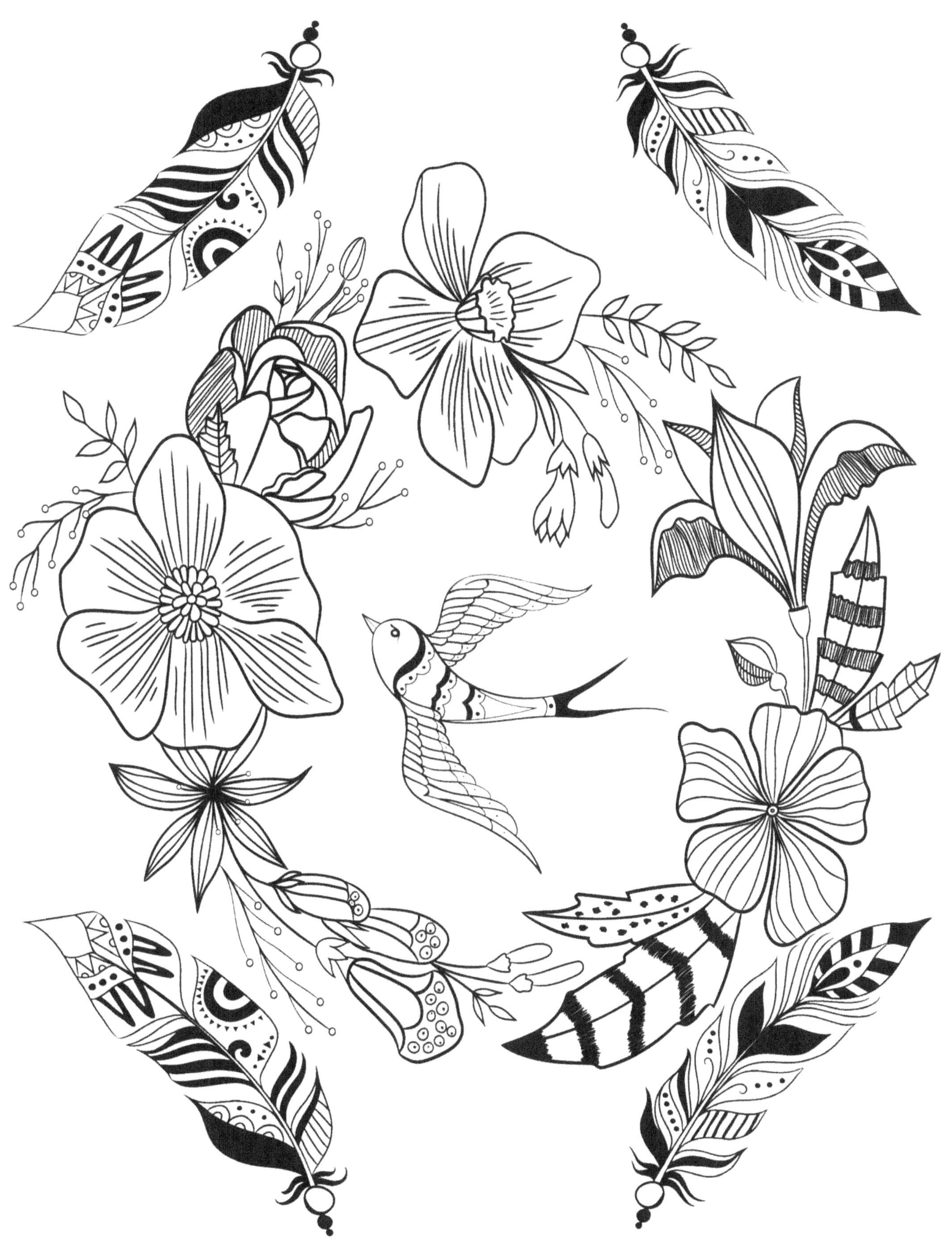

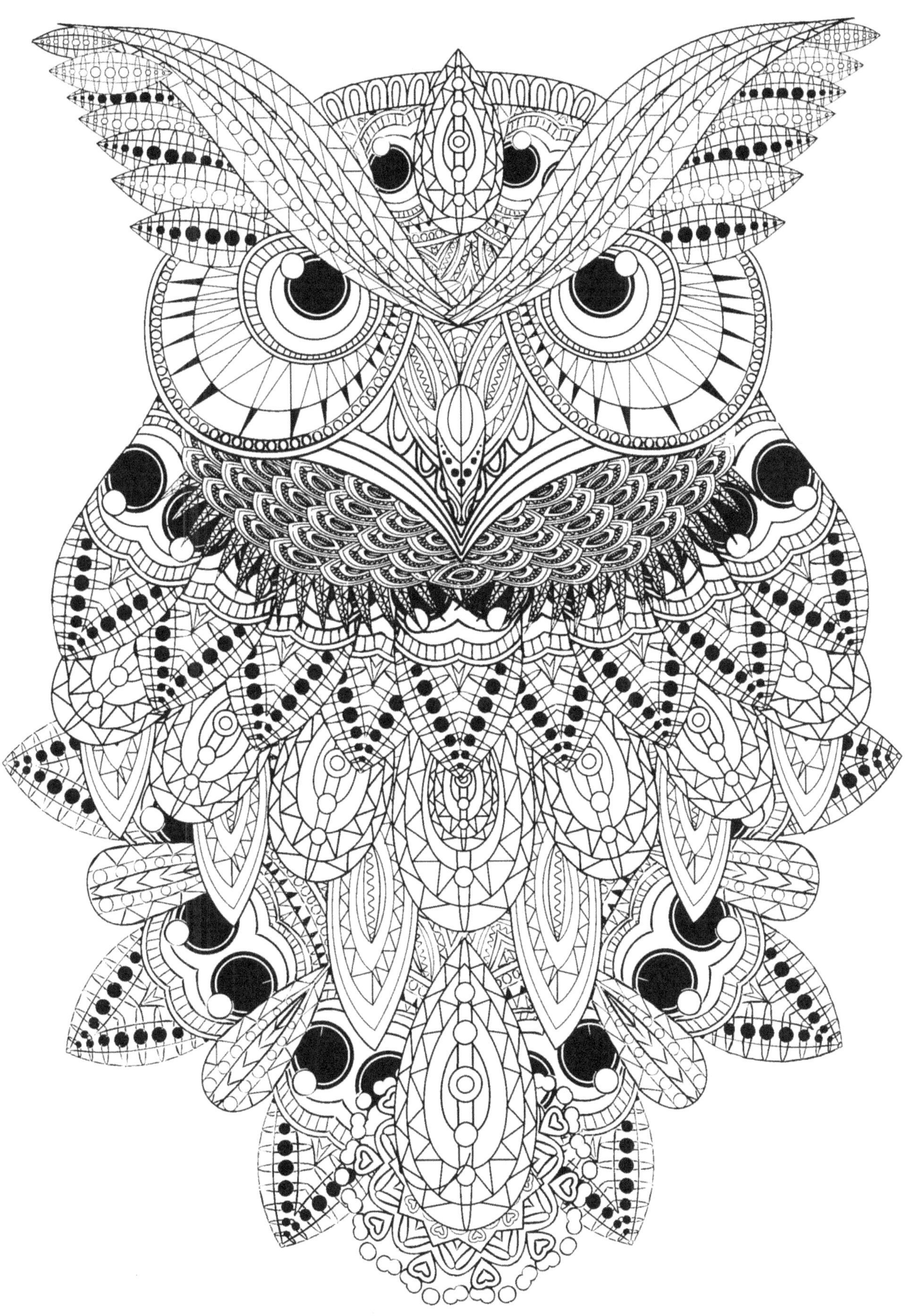

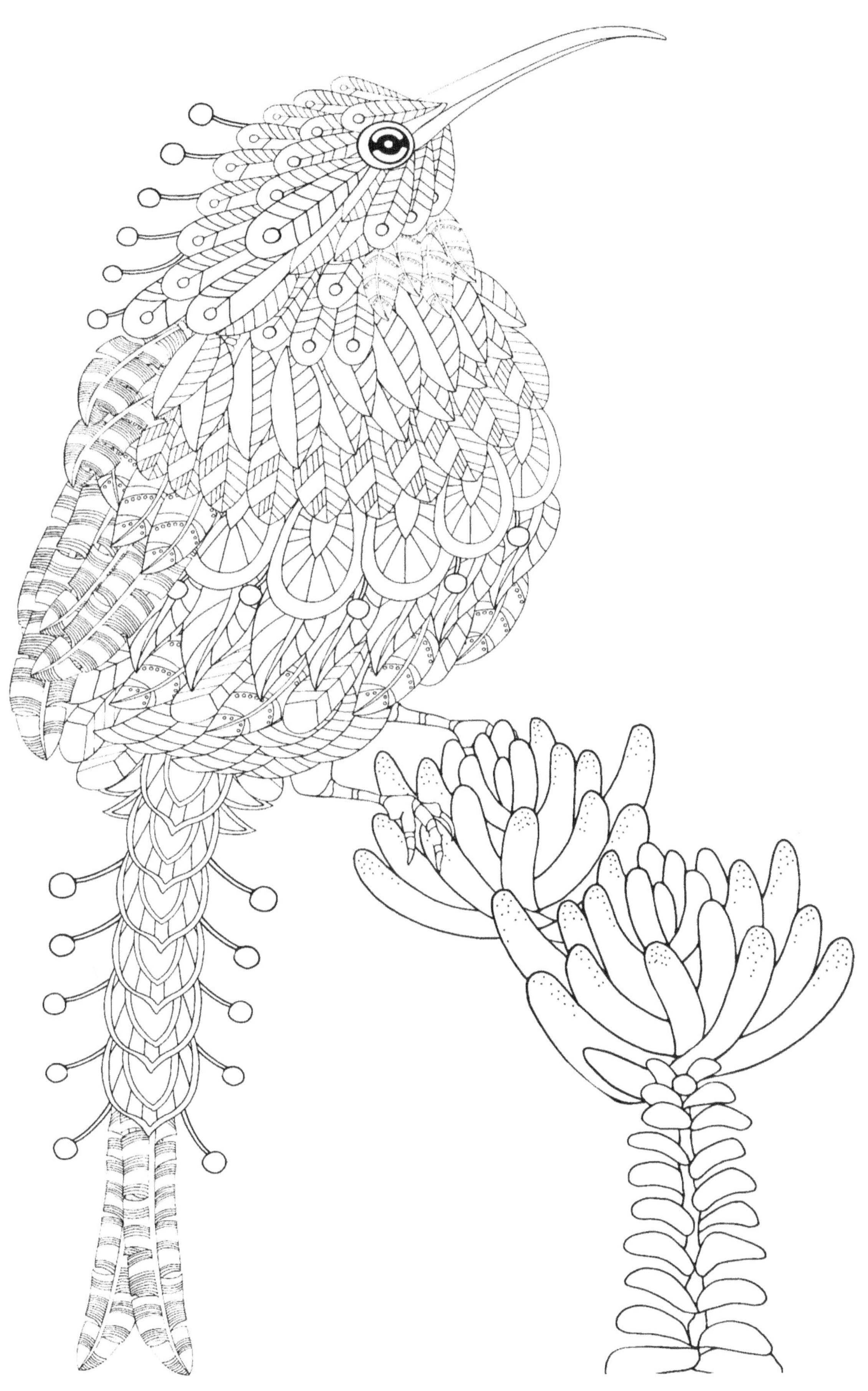

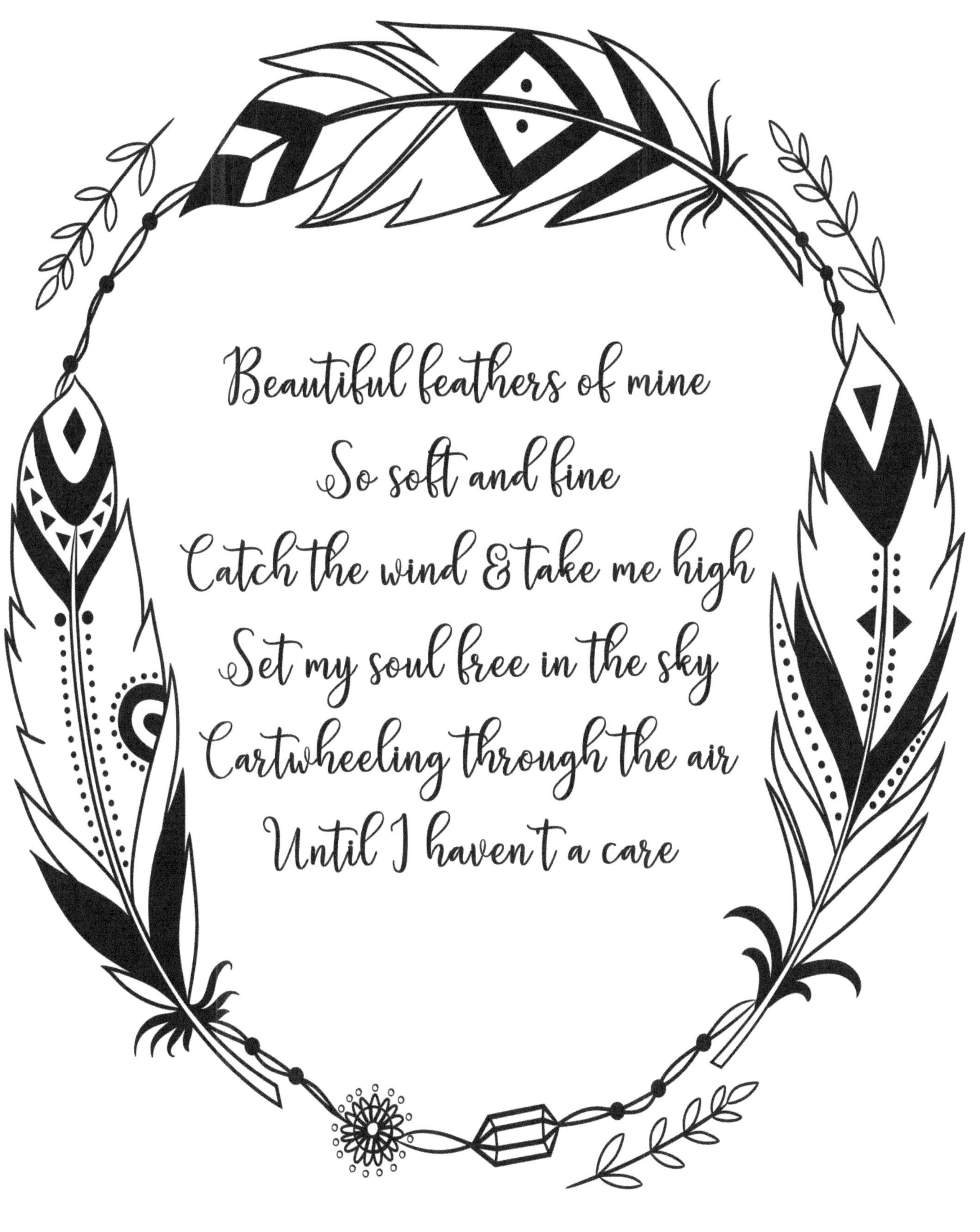

Beautiful feathers of mine
So soft and fine
Catch the wind & take me high
Set my soul free in the sky
Cartwheeling through the air
Until I haven't a care